Spillin' the Beans

Spillin' the Beans

BEHIND THE SCENES AT L. L. BEAN

CARLENE GRIFFIN
—— A 45-Year Employee ——

Second Printing

© 1992 by Carlene Griffin

Library of Congress Catalog Card Number: 93-90057

ISBN: 0-9635996-3-1

Cover and text design by AMY FISCHER DESIGN, Camden, Maine.

Cover photograph of Carlene Griffin by JEFF STEVENSEN, Portland, Maine

Interior illustrations by CHRIS VAN DUSEN, Camden, Maine

Produced by AMY FISCHER DESIGN, Camden, Maine

Editorial services by WARREN PUBLISHING SERVICES, Eastport, Maine

Printed and bound by KNOWLTON & MCLEARY PRINTING, Farmington, Maine

This book is dedicated to Leon Leonwood Bean and Leon A. Gorman. They've made it possible for me to look back on a lifetime career without a moment's regret.

Contents

NOTICE

I do not consider a sale complete until goods are worn out and customer still satisfied.

We will thank anyone to return goods that are not perfectly satisfactory.

Should the person reading this notice know of anyone who is not satisfied with our goods, I will consider it a favor to be notified.

Above all things we wish to avoid having a dissatisfied customer.

This notice in a 1916 L. L. Bean circular sets the tone for the company's dealings with customers. It had been that way since 1912 and continues without change to this day.

Preface

This book is of, for and by the employees of L. L. Bean—employee memories and anecdotes going back as far as sixty years ago and some as recent as this year—recorded or written by the employees themselves with no holds barred. And what would Leon Leonwood Bean have thought of all this? I think he would have approved of it in an instant.

In his autobiography, *My Story*, L. L. Bean writes as follows:

> In 1918, I took out two United States patents and one Canadian patent relating to the back seam and reinforcement in the tongue. [This was a modification to the famous L. L. Bean Hunting Shoe.] In the meantime, I had hired Hazel Goldrup, the daughter of my cutter and stitcher. At this point in my story, I wish to state that Miss Goldrup deserves more credit for the success of my mail-order business in the early years than any other one person. She was the bookkeeper, cashier, auditor and boss of the office. When I went on my hunting trips, I never worried about the office.

In fact, L. L. Bean does nearly as much talking about his employees in his autobiography as he does about himself. His feelings for them were warm and genuinely appreciative; he respected and wanted their views, and I have no doubt he would have welcomed and enjoyed the many reminiscences that follow. It was an attitude that made working for this man one of the great joys of my life, and as he went out of his way to credit part of his early success to an employee, so do I gladly credit a long, very happy and very productive working career to L. L. Bean.

After L. L. Bean's death in 1967, he was succeeded by Leon Gorman who

Early photo of L. L. Bean just after arriving in Freeport.

has "filled" L. L.'s hunting shoes in the same open-handed spirit. As one very old-time employee put it, "Leon Gorman is so much like L. L. Bean, it's scary!" The sheer size of today's L. L. Bean Company and its attendant growth and modernization under Leon Gorman continue to amaze this forty-five-year employee, but there has been no change in the company's relations with its employees. L. L. Bean's famous 100% guarantee encompasses not only the company's products, but also the unique bond between management and all the rest of us. It is a good place to work. Believe me.

L. L. Bean was, without question, one of this nation's leading merchants, and his company's operations were studied and analyzed by many, including the Harvard Business School. Whatever such studies may reveal about successful business management (including employee relations), my purpose is to tell you the company's story as *we* lived it behind the counters and in the back rooms.

It may not be as instructive as a business analysis, but I promise you it will be a lot more fun.

Acknowledgments

Without my daughter Jamie's encouragement and unwavering support, this project would never have come to fulfillment. The writing is by Fred Bell, working from my many transcripts and notes, and the design and production are by Amy Fischer. Jamie kept me at it, and Fred and Amy made it happen. I love you all.

In the mid-eighties, William David Barry and Bruce Kennett were invited by Leon Gorman, president of L. L. Bean, Inc., to produce a "scrapbook" based on information from company files and archives. The result was a priceless historical volume on the company entitled, *L. L. Bean, Inc., Outdoor Sporting Specialties—A Company Scrapbook*, privately printed for L. L. Bean, Inc., by The Anthoensen Press, Portland, Maine, in 1987.

When I set about the serious business of recording the anecdotes and personal reminiscences for this manuscript, it became necessary to frequently "set the scene" for the reader's better understanding. This, in turn, required the use of company photographs, newspaper and magazine clippings about the company and other related archival materials. Had it not been for Barry and Kennett's exhaustive and remarkable research for their Scrapbook, and particularly for their superb acumen in selecting newspaper clippings from the vast amount of source material available to them, my work would have been immeasurably more difficult.

L. L. BEAN, INC.

from 1912 to 1992

1912   L. L. Bean invented the Maine Hunting Shoe in 1911, but it wasn't until 1912 that he sent out his first advertising circular and established the mail-order foundation for his business.

1924   Sales reached $135,000, and 25 people were on the L. L. Bean payroll. The catalog, which accounted for the vast majority of sales, was beginning to take on its present look and included many hunting, fishing and camping items.

The thirties   These were the watershed years for the company. The Great Depression destroyed thousands of U.S. companies, but L. L. Bean not only survived, it enjoyed phenomenal growth, expanding its operations space five different times during the decade and exceeding the million-dollar mark in sales in 1937. L. L. Bean's functional, no-nonsense clothing and equipment, worth every penny charged, seemed a good bargain to tens of thousands of people in the Depression years, and it was during these hard times that the company's reputation was established both nationally and internationally.

World War II   The Maine Hunting Shoe was adapted for use by both the army and navy. Several other items were made for the armed forces. Mr. Bean and other company executives spent much time in Washington as consultants.

1946   The company was featured in a long article in *The Saturday Evening Post*, which was then the nation's leading weekly magazine. Nineteen thousand catalog requests were generated by that one article. Other articles about the company were featured in *Life*, *Forbes* and the *Reader's Digest* during the forties, as well as in several newspapers.

The fifties   Sales reached the two-million mark in 1950. Twenty-four-hour service was inaugurated. A ladies department was established. The company was catering to the needs of family recreation as well as hunting and fishing. The L. L. Bean catalog carried 104 pages of advertising in 1955 and prompted over 90% of all sales.

The sixties   Mr. Bean was nearing ninety at the beginning of the decade and although his company's reputation was at its highest peak, its operations had grown stagnant and facilities were outdated. Sales remained at about the two-million-dollar level. Much needed to be changed and updated to accommodate the new leisure-time markets and computerized business methods of competitors. Following the death of Mr. Bean in 1967, his son Carl took over the firm but died suddenly several month later. Leon Gorman was named president.

From the sixties to the present   Under Mr. Gorman's presidency, the company computerized and adopted the many changes necessary to increase its competitiveness and serve a market that has grown in quantum leaps. From about $2 million in sales in 1960, for example, the company's 1991 sales exceeded $628 million. One hundred and twenty million catalogs were mailed last year to 15 million recipients. These are figures the founder probably could not have conceived of, yet have been realized while faithfully adhering to Mr. L. L. Bean's business and personal ethics. Operations methods were changed, but the character and spirit of the company remained as they were in 1912. As an employee who first joined the company in 1935, I have witnessed the changes that have occurred at Bean's, but I have also witnessed the keeping of the qualities that have so endeared the company to its millions of customers. A big family has no less love and integrity in it than a small family, and throughout all the vast changes in operations, these qualities have remained constant. It is this that sets this company apart—and will continue to do so.

Introduction

A boy growing up in Freeport, here in Maine, as I did would know L. L. Bean as he would know anybody else in so small a place. I may have known him a little better than some, because he bought three ducks from me every fall. I kept a flock of domesticated mallards, which were still lawful live "tollers" in the 1920s and 1930s, and as the season for waterfowl approached L. L. would remind me to fetch him a trio. A drake and two hens. These would be tethered, or anchored, before his duck blind with the two females to one side and the drake to the other. This arrangement was based on the eternal verities. When a flock of wild birds came over, the anchored drake would put up a big hullabaloo lest the wild gentlemen approach his two tethered females, and the two tethered females would put up a similar hullabaloo lest they wouldn't. Mr. Bean (and any other duck hunter) would take advantage of this mating urge and come home each evening with the limit. Mr. Bean paid me one dollar for each toller.

I have no idea what it was like to be a girl-child growing up in Mr. Bean's Freeport. Carlene Groves Griffin can tell you as you read along. Her daddy, Carl Groves, didn't get a boy—hence, Carlene. She lived down Bow Street, on the right side of the tracks, and here is her story of a lifetime with the L. L. Bean mail-order business. As every one of we old-time Freeporters well knows, the gracious days are long gone and things in town are not the same. Let Carlene tell about it.

JOHN GOULD
Freeport High School, class of 1926
Friendship, Maine, 1992

1

Unconditional Love and Other Customer Benefits

Charlie Smith—I think it was Charlie Smith—was answering one of the customer-service phones one night and got this call from a lady in New York. It was during the woodstove craze, probably the early seventies, when oil prices had gone berserk and using woodstoves had become the thing. Everybody, everywhere, wanted a woodstove, and this lady had bought hers at Bean's. The problem was that it smoked and she wanted the stove replaced.

Charlie: Do you have the flue adjusted properly? The problem might be the down draft in the chimney.

Lady: Flue?

Charlie: You know . . . that little handle on the stovepipe.

Lady: Well, I don't have a stovepipe.

Charlie: You don't have a stovepipe? You know, the pipe that goes from the stove into the wall and connects with the chimney.

Lady: No, I don't have any pipe. I build a fire in the stove and the room fills with smoke.

Charlie: Lady, send your stove back. We'll give you back your money.

I remember the lady who bought a Christmas wreath at Bean's and called us up because it had turned brown.

Customer Service Rep: That's terrible. When did you buy it? I'll look up the order and replace it right away.

Customer: Let's see. Last year about . . .

Rep: Last year?

Customer: Yes, I don't understand it. It was green when I got it and now it's brown.

Rep: What did you do?

Customer: Well, I stored it. I wanted it for this year, too.

Rep: Well, that wreath is the real stuff. You can't . . . it doesn't store, you know. You have to buy another one.

Customer (very uptight)*:* I never would have bought this wreath if I'd known that. I need to hang it up tomorrow. What do you suggest I do?

Rep: We'll wire you $25 right now . . . and you go out and buy another wreath.

And Bean's did exactly that.

The love affair between L. L. Bean's and its customers—and that's what it is, a love affair—is based on a lot more than Bean's legendary 100% product guarantee. It's based on Bean's 100% guarantee to understand and sympathize with customers. Now, a company can instill that spirit in employees only up to a certain point—beyond that, the instinct and genes of the employee have to take over, and I can tell you from forty-five years of experience with Bean's that its employees have just about cornered the market on nice-people genes. If a customer even *thinks* the company hasn't done right by him (or her), everybody who hears about it at Bean's will be concerned—no matter what the facts may be or how unreasonable the complaint—and this concern comes from the heart. I'm talking about telephone operators, clerks, customer service representatives, department managers and on up to the top. As I said, you can't *program* understanding and a caring attitude into employees; you can't train people to put themselves into an unreasonable customers' position, understand where the customer is coming from, sympathize with the situation and then solve the problem in a way the customer feels is right and proper. No, this sort of empathy and genuine caring for people has to be inside an employee and come out spontaneously. It is this kind of employee—by the hundreds—that has helped spawn the loyalties between the L. L. Bean Company and its millions of friends and customers. Here's a little verbatim conversation with one of our ex-telephone operators, Anna Williams, while we were sitting around gabbing and playing with the tape recorder one afternoon. This book is about Bean's employees, after all, and this conversation will give you a good insight into the caliber of people we have working with us.

Me: When did you go to work for Bean's?

Anna: In '51. They put me on the typing list, then into Bookkeeping, and, oh, my Lord, it was awful dull and sedate. Very nice people, but dull, dull, dull. Of course, I was eager to keep any job I could get and I worked and worked and I had this awful ego, thinking everyone was watching me and talking about me, of course, but they weren't paying any attention.

Me: It's always that way on a new job.

Anna: Well, I was scared to death. I got so nervous one time—I had worked overtime—that when I ran down the steps to get in my friend's car (he always waited for me), I just jumped in the back and sat there. It was dark, remember. After a while, this old guy in the driver's seat turned around. I'd never seen him before. He sort of smiled at me, you know, and said, "Why don't you stay awhile?" I got out of there real fast, I can tell you.

Me: Sounds like a few fellas I know. What else happened while you were in Bookkeeping?

Anna: Well, they were an intellectual bunch up there. They all had their favorite actors and singers and writers and speakers, and I felt like a dunce. I had to come up with *somebody*. I had seen *King Solomon's Mines* with Stewart Granger, so I came in talking about this wonderful Stewart Granger person. And I went on and on about it—very intellectually, of course—while I was writing out these refund checks. Sure enough, about a month later we got one of the checks back from somebody in Chicago. I'd made it out to Stewart Granger. Well, I thought it was hilarious. I laughed my head off—and I made up my mind not to try and be intellectual anymore.

Me: Was it after that they put you on the switchboard?

Anna: Yes. And I loved that new job. I was right at the center of everything, and I talked with all kinds of people.

Me: Did you handle complaints?

Anna: I'd get a complaint once in a while. One morning, my very first call was from a guy swearing and hollering. So I said, "Mister, now what's your name?" And he gave me his name and address, and it was about a back-ordered chamois shirt. I said, "Well, just a minute, sir, just a minute. You hold on. I think I know about that order." So I looked it up, and of course the poor fellow had called in before—this was his fifth call—so I said, "I don't blame you for being upset. This is the fifth call you have made on this shirt, and Mr. Bean is upset over this situation. We're all upset over it. And there's nothing I can do except promise you that yours will be the very first order to go out when the shirts come in. And I will personally see to it." Well, he calmed down right away. No more swearing and yelling. "Now," I said, "there's one thing I'd like to know, because I'm sure you were brought up as a gentleman, so you must not be feeling well—to talk to a lady the way you did. So what is the trouble?" And I was sincere, too. I said, "What is the trouble?" And he said, "I just ache all over and I'm sick." I said,

Anna Williams.

"I know. I could tell that's why you did that. You scoot over to a doctor right quick and get straightened around. And you're going to get your shirt before you know it." And, by gosh, I was lucky. The shirt came in the very next day, and I mailed it right out.

Me: Sounds like he really needed a doctor.

Anna: I was hoping he'd call back so I could see how he was making out. I also had a lady who called right at noon, usually once a week, sometimes twice a week, and she'd give me descriptions of her dog kennel—she'd tell me who was having pups and who wasn't and that sort of thing.

Me: She just needed someone to talk to?

Anna: That's right. I really loved talking with her. And I loved working

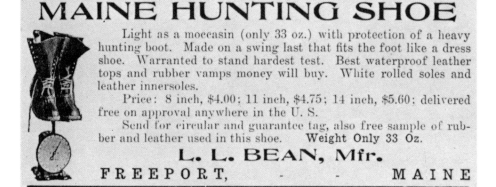

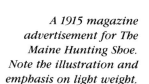

A 1915 magazine advertisement for The Maine Hunting Shoe. Note the illustration and emphasis on light weight.

at Bean's. I'll always have very fond memories of Bean's. They were good to their customers and they were good to the help. There was only one employee I met at Bean's who was never satisfied. I won't mention his name, but he was never happy with anything . . . not with Mr. Bean, not with the store, not with anything or anybody . . . the proverbial griper. He was a wonderful carpenter, so he just needed something to gripe about, you know. Anyway, he'd come in griping, and I always kept two jars of pickles for him in my drawer and I'd say, "Here, have a pickle and tell me all about your troubles; you'll feel better." So, he'd tell me and he'd feel better.

There's no company training program that can instill the spirit and attitude of an Anna Williams into its employees; only God can do that . . . and I can tell you Bean's is filled with Anna Williamses. Now you know where the customers' love affair with this company comes from.

The official date for the start of the L. L. Bean Company is given as 1912, but L. L.'s creation of the Maine Hunting Shoe, which launched his career, came about in 1911, and the shoe was in small-scale production during that year. In his book, *My Story*, published in 1960, L. L. writes as follows:

> Every year I made up a hunting party to go to Wild River, New Hampshire . . . In fact, I was much more interested in hunting than in running the store. [At that time, he worked in his brother Ervin's clothing store in Freeport.] I was also quite interested in getting the right kind of footwear for deer hunting.
>
> In 1911, I decided after a hunting trip that the shoes I was wearing were no good. Born and bred in the Oxford Hills [of Maine] the wood trails were no novelty to me . . . I grew tired of wearing shoes that hurt my feet. I took a pair of shoe rubbers from the stock on the shelves [in his brother's store] and had a shoe-maker cut out a pair of 7½″ leather tops. The local cobbler stitched the whole thing together.
>
> I quite innocently praised my new shoe to a prospective customer, Edgar Conant, who came to the store. In September, 1911, I made a pair for him to try out. From his recommendation, I decided I had struck the right thing in the great hunting ground state of Maine.
>
> I made up and sold one hundred pairs at $3.50 a pair, using a regular shoe rubber by filling in the heel with pieces of felt. The idea was all right, but the rubber was not strong enough to hold the stitched-on tops. Ninety pairs were returned and the money was refunded.

Mr. Bean borrowed money from Otho, another of his four brothers, went to Boston and arranged for the U.S. Rubber Company to supply him with a light rubber sole strong enough to hold the attached leather tops. When that was accomplished, including the borrowing of more money to defray the cost, he at last had the L. L. Bean Maine Hunting Shoe that eventually became what is undoubtedly the most famous brand-name footwear in history for sports enthusiasts.

An early photo of Ted Goldrup, L. L. Bean's first employee.

Various modifications were made to the shoe in succeeding years, and it became so popular with out-of-town people who happened to stop in the store that Mr. Bean experimented with mail order to reach a wider market. It wasn't long before mail-order sales far outstripped the relatively little business he could realize from a retail counter, and by January of 1918 he had made the decision to concentrate entirely on this more profitable method of selling. He leased the top floor of a building in Freeport and was now on his own as "L. L. Bean, Manufacturer." His company had been born—and the "Manufacturer" part had a lot to do with the Goldrups.

In the Preface to this book, I mentioned Mr. Bean's praise for Hazel Goldrup, the new company's "boss of the office." Hazel was the daughter of Ted and Gertrude Goldrup, both of whom also worked for the new company. Kippy Goldrup, Hazel's brother, born in 1904—and who also worked for L. L. Bean—still has sharp memories of his family's contributions to the business:

Kippy: My father was L. L.'s leather cutter, and every day he'd take the patterns and the leather and the orders and he'd wrap them in brown paper . . . and then shove the package under the wagon seat and bring it all home for my mother to stitch. I don't know how many nights she had to stay up, burning the midnight oil. You see, we didn't have any electricity in those days . . . she literally worked under an oil lamp. And, of course, Mr. Bean's business got bigger and bigger and the hours for my mother got longer and longer, but I never heard her complain for a moment. She just worked on the leather, of course, stitching it together and sewing on the L. L. Bean label; a cobbler attached the leather to the rubber sole. She had a White sewing machine. I think it's on display somewhere at the company, and I can tell you I saw it smoke many a night from all the stitching of that leather. And then, of course, the next morning, or whenever my mother had some bundles ready, I'd take them over to Bean's. It was only a three-mile walk. And I remember my mother had a clock to keep track of her work hours, right to the minute, and then Mr. Bean would pay her for the time she said she worked. There was never any question about it, of course. Later on, when she couldn't keep up with the work, there was so much of it, you see, she went to work over at the company factory. They used to work some overtime, I'll tell you. I remember one week we earned a hundred dollars, and I want you to know that was quite a thing in those days. Boy, I'll tell you, you get me thinking about those old days and you can be sure Mr. Bean had quite a team going for him. Everybody liked everybody else, and we put out the best work a human being is capable of. We made very, very fine hunting shoes and we were as proud of them as Mr. Bean was. If anything went wrong with a shoe we took it personally and got to the bottom of it in a hurry. I hear it's the same now, even though I hardly recognize the place. I mean the quality work and everything is the same.

Me: You bet it is, Kippy. Hasn't changed a bit.

"Win" Given started with L. L. Bean in 1917. This photo is from 1951. (Courtesy Guy Gannett Publishing Co.)

In assembling the material for this book, I sent out a questionnaire to many of the past and present employees of the company. I asked them for anecdotes, employment information and other data, but somehow I overlooked asking them about their opinions of the company and how they felt about working there. They took care of that omission for me. Many of the respondents took the time to spontaneously and voluntarily add a sentence or two about the pleasure it was to work for L. L. Bean, Inc. Here are just a few examples—and they are typical of the many:

Sure was a real nice company to work for. L. L. and Carl (L. L. Bean's son) were always so fair with their help. I miss working—especially the folks I worked with. I really know the difference, for I had worked in some other local shoe factories. I am really proud to tell people I had worked at Bean's so many years.

The only comment I could say is that L. L. Bean's is a family-concerned outfit. They care about people. It was a pleasant experience.

I enjoyed working at L. L. Bean because—one of several reasons—we all seemed to be one happy family . . .

A WONDERFUL PLACE TO WORK!!!

. . . L. L. Bean has been, and will be, a great part of our lives. I feel fortunate that my family has had the good fortune to be able to work there.

If L. L. Bean had been alive, and if I had sent a questionnaire to him, I have no doubt he would have just as spontaneously and voluntarily added a sentence or two that credited his employees for making all the good things possible.

And just let me add this last penned-in note on one of my returned questionnaires . . . from a forty-year employee:

. . . As you well know, I have great love and respect for the company, for our customers, and for everyone that has worked for L. L. Bean.

"Love," that respondent said.

And that's what it's all about.

It's honest, it's genuine . . . and our customers feel it right down to the toes of their Maine Hunting Shoes.

2

Men at Work

*F*or many years, Russell Dyer was the head maintenance man at the L. L. Bean Company. He had a couple of helpers—Everett Bucklin and Raymie Estabrook come to mind—and he may have had one or two others from time to time, but it was a small crew in any event and they were responsible for keeping the building running. It was the only building we had in those days.

Russell was like his boss, L. L. Bean, in that he was practical and down-to-earth. He had his own ideas about things, and his talents were such that he was eventually lured away by a big company in Portland. Anyway, he came home from work one day (as his neighbor, Jim Palmer, puts it), "Just beside himself." The building he was responsible for was to have a new ventilating and heating system, and he had sat in on the meeting with the engineering "experts."

The southerly side of this building was all glass, and Russell spent two hours at the meeting while the experts talked about this control and that control, both heating and ventilating coming out of the same system. Russell didn't like what he heard, and when he'd finally had enough of it, he spoke up:

Russell: Excuse me, but I've been over the budget for this project, and I don't see any allowance in here for paperweights.

Expert: For what?

Russell: Paperweights.

Expert: What do paperweights have to do with the subject we're discussing?

Russell: Well, the way I look at it . . . considering the way your system is designed . . . when you get a day in January, a bright, sunny day where the temperature outside is about fifteen degrees below zero, the south side of this building with the sun beating in is going to be about ninety-five degrees before you turn your system on. The north side of the building will be in the shade. If my calculations are correct, there is going to be about a forty-knot wind blowing from one side of this building to the other. And I think you are going to need paperweights.

The "experts" promptly went back to their drawing boards and redesigned their system to automatically adjust for severe temperature variables within the building. Russell, as always, had the company's interests in mind, just as he had always had L. L.'s interests in mind.

The Yankee ingenuity, hard work and common sense of L. L. Bean's employees were responsible for the development of better working conditions, more efficient manufacturing processes, better shipping, handling and storage methods and many new products and cost-saving systems in many departments. Freeman Condon, for example, noted the special problems with smoothing out innersoles—a long, hard, wearisome task that ruined the hands of the lady workers. After thinking about it a bit he went to the Lisbon dump, scavenged up a washing machine and designed a system that not only did the job better and faster, but kept the ladies' hands looking like ladies' hands. Maurice Hilton had a job that entailed the measuring, marking and cutting of rope that came in 1200-foot coils. He had to do that job with a marker and a pair of scissors—a long, costly process. Becoming disgusted, he adapted an eyelet machine to the task that cut the time in half and made the job a lot easier. Carl Bean's list of manufacturing and systems improvements would fill a small book. L. L. Bean, himself, was of the same inventive mind, creating several original products for the company and improving many that were offered to him by other manufacturers before he'd allow the products to be put in his catalog. He recognized and attracted people with functional, no-nonsense ingenuity, both men and women, and in countless ways, after he'd hired them, they made his growing company a considerably more efficient and better place to work. There is George Soule, for instance . . .

George worked for the company and was a friend of L. L.'s in the early days. He and L. L. frequently went duck hunting, but they seldom found anything to shoot.

George: I had the worst-looking decoys you ever saw in your life. So I told L. L. one day that I could make a better decoy. I didn't know that for a fact, but I thought I could, and, by golly, I did. I went down to Portland and found an old refrigeration truck they were taking apart, and this truck had cork in it. I took the cork home and made some decoys. They were pretty crude, but the next time L. L. and I went duck hunting, we shot a lot of ducks. L. L. said, "Well, George, I've got a catalog. I've seen with my own eyes that you have something here, so if you want to make decoys, I'll put 'em in my catalog." Well, that's just what I did, and that's just what he did, and, of course, you can be sure I was making decoys a lot better in a few weeks. The company is still making decoys with a cork body—and the first one came out of that refrigeration truck.

Having established himself as the premier decoy-maker for Bean's, hunters would come in occasionally and ask George for special kinds of decoys.

George: A lawyer came in one day and asked for a set of oversized decoys. Now, there's nothing new about oversized decoys—they've been around a hundred years or more—but I hadn't made any and it was an interesting new project for me. So I said, "All right. I'll make them." And I did. He came back a few weeks later, looked at the set of decoys I'd made and said they were fine, just what he wanted. I said, "You know, they look pretty big to me. If they don't work, bring them back and I'll put goose heads on them or something." He said, "Oh, don't worry about them. They'll be fine." He had a place down on Merrymeeting Bay, and apparently he'd go out there early in the morning and go hunting with these big decoys. He'd draw all the ducks around. He'd shoot his limit, leave the decoys where they were, then go back up to his house and sit on his porch or maybe go off to Portland for all I knew. The main point of this is that after drawing all the ducks he could shoot, he'd leave the decoys where they were, right in the water. Well . . . another man, Ranson Kelley, lived up at the mouth of the Kennebec River and he fancied himself the biggest and best duck hunter around. One day he came to see me and asked if I'd made the oversized decoys for the lawyer. I said I had, and Ranson said, "Make me two dozen." I asked him why. He said, "Why? I'll tell you why! All those ducks migrating into Merrymeeting Bay, coming right down the Kennebec River, they come right over my place and they spot those big decoys of yours at the lawyer's and they light out over there! And all the while that lawyer's up there, sitting on his porch and drinking coffee! Those ducks, they come into his place by the hundreds!" Ranson was fuming as he told me the story. So I made him the big decoys, and not long afterward L. L. put these in the catalog, too, and they really sold like crazy.

Justin Williams was another long-time employee at Bean's, and like George Soule, he accompanied L. L. on many of his duck-hunting adventures. On this particular occasion, L. L., Justin and Danny Snow were waiting for the ducks to come in and, as usual, there wasn't much activity.

Justin: I had this old duck-call that I got around 1938 or so—one of the best ever made. Of course, L. L. didn't know that. He didn't know much about duck-calls and didn't have them in his catalog. But I was brought up on a farm and had hunted ducks all my life, and I knew what this particular duck-call could do and I knew how to use it. Some duck-calls say, "Well, the feeding isn't so good over here." Other duck-calls say, "The feeding's great and come on in." You have to know what a duck-call says. It takes a little experience and luck to get a good one, and, like I said, this was the best I'd ever used. Anyway, L. L. and Danny were in one blind and I was in another with the dog. So I got this old duck-call out and used it. Now, I want you to understand that I'm not exaggerating here. Within a few minutes there must have been 500 ducks flying around the blinds. I mean, the sky was *filled* with ducks, different kinds of ducks, all milling around. Honest to God, you never saw such a tangle! L. L. was standing there in shock, and til' the day he died, he never got over it. You can believe that the next fall he had duck-calls in his catalog, and he had George Soule make them. George's calls were patterned after the one I had used that day. Anyway, that's how Bean's got into duck-calls. You had to demonstrate things for L. L. He wasn't about to sell anything that hadn't been field-tested to his satisfaction. And I bet there's a few thousand duck-hunters out there who are equally satisfied with the duck-calls they got from the catalog.

The practical knowledge and inventive nature of the employees Mr. Bean hired weren't the only contributions they made to the company. Many of them offered much more than that—a unique brand of common sense and

Freeport Square in the early thirties.

special feelings and appreciations that could only be derived from a background of hard, serious work in Maine fields and woods. It was the kind of growing-up that breeds a deep reverence for nature and its creatures—it is very distinct—and you'll get a sense of what I mean from these further words of Justin Williams; you'll also be closer to understanding why L. L. Bean's is unique not only because of its founder, but also because of the character and traits of the people he put to work for the company.

Justin: Let's see. I was the fourth boy, and I was the one who would go out at four or four-thirty in the morning and feed the horses and cattle before we could ask them for a day's work. When I went through the barn, I'd always stop and talk to the horses and pat them and what-not, you know. And if I happened to overlook my usual greeting to a couple of them, they'd make quite a commotion, pawing the floor and snorting. Some people think animals are dumb, but they're not so dumb. I was riding the hay rake one day when I was up on Beech Hill, and, of course, I was on an old metal seat. The horse was an old mare named Maggie. Well, I slipped off the seat, fell right behind her heels and was caught up in the hay, being rolled over and over. I said, "Whoa, Maggie. Whoa!" I can see those old hind feet now . . . Boom! Boom! Boom!—and they stopped, just like that. And those metal tines were just bouncing right up and down. Most of the time, you tell a horse to "whoa" and she'll take a few steps, you know. Not this time. Not one extra step. Maggie knew.

Me: I bet you loved that old horse.

Justin: Love for animals? You'd better believe I had love for animals. Whenever a horse would pass on, you know, I'd go to the funeral. They'd usually take them out at daybreak, so nobody would be around, but I'd get word of it and attend the funeral and pay my respects to the horse. I think every young person should have a taste of farm life, if for no other reason than to learn a little about animals. They're a lot like us in their emotions, and to experience that is humbling and very real. If you know about animals, you know a lot about people.

Me: I think that's very true.

Justin: Sure. Let me tell you about the bull. This was the only animal I can remember who hated me on sight. He was a little on the rough side, and he just took it in his head not to like me and that was that. People can sometimes be that way, too, you know. It doesn't matter how nice you may be to them, they just don't like you. It started when my brother, Dean, and I took on the job of rounding up the cows every day and bringing them in to milk. My best buddy, an old collie dog, always came with us, and one day the bull decided he wasn't going to go with the cows; he was going to come after Don or me or the collie. As he charged us, the collie grabbed the bull by the throat and gave us time to get out of the pasture. Anyway, after the bull tried to nail me two or three more times, I figured I didn't like him a hell of a lot, either. There was a carriage house right next to the fence where the bull was in pasture. In fact, the fence came right up to the side of the carriage house and part of the fence was painted on the house. Now, this house had a stone basement and there was a high window above it where we used to dry our beans. This one particular day the bull was pawing the ground near the sand-and-gravel pit we had in the field and he was bellowing at me as usual, so I went out in my bare feet and kicked some sand in his face. He started for me, and I ran to the carriage house where I'd left the window open. I jumped up on the stones, grabbed the window sill and pulled myself up. Just about the time I got my legs in, KAJUNG! went the old bull into the stone foundation.

Me (with a twinkle): I thought you loved animals.

Justin: It was a game, you know. And we played it a few times after that. But, my God! the last time I did it, my mother was standing there! Honest to God, she was just as white as she could be. She was scared to death!

Me: And that was the last time . . .

Justin: Yes. We stayed out of the pasture after that. Jack and I—Jack was the collie—we did everything together. When the work was done, we'd go up the Pownal Road to the big pines over there and sit down somewhere and see what was going on. We'd sit still and hear deer and birds, and sometimes fox and partridge. Once, when Dad was out lumbering, one of the cows aborted and I called Dr. Anderson. He taught Jack and me how to give them epsom salts and warm water out of an old Moxie bottle and how to hold the cow's head and how to go in and bring out the afterbirth to avoid infection. I tell you, it's an experience when you can make an animal feel better, and I'm sure that if old Jack had had a thumb and fingers he'd have been able to take care of the next cow that aborted.

Me: You hunted a lot with L. L., didn't you?

Justin: Oh, yes. He was quite a hunter in his own right. He didn't use some of the techniques others did, but when you're around animals and birds long enough you sharpen up anyhow. You know what they like and how they'll react. I've been hunting with other people who get their limit by eight-thirty or so and they want to keep right on shooting. Ducks or deer or whatever, they're not satisfied. They have to have more. L. L. was never like that. He was a good man to hunt with. You know, you don't have a garden unless you leave something for seed. You don't have animals or birds unless you leave the ones that produce. And you have to take care of the places where animals and birds live. If youngsters go by those axioms, there'll always be something around, whether it's game we're talking about or woods and lakes and streams. Game management and environmental protection aren't new, you know, not to hunters and fishermen, at least. It's just that many people are reckless and unthinking. Now you see why I think it would be a good idea for young people to spend some time on a farm and in the woods and fields. It's more than a vacation. It's a learning experience that benefits us all in the long run. It's not talking to the animals and birds that's so important. It's just the other way around. It's the animals and birds talking to *us.*

There you have Justin Williams.

And if you had been a hunter or fisherman calling Bean's for some small word of advice not too many years ago, the operator could just as easily have turned you over to Justin as anyone else. You wouldn't have known Justin from Adam, but you'd quickly sense that, whoever this man was, he was worth listening to and that you could trust what he said without any qualification whatever.

Bean's has had that reputation since the first day it opened for business. And among the major reasons for it is the singular caliber of the people hired by the company. It really wouldn't have made much difference who the operator might have connected you with. The expertise of the person you were talking with, the philosophy, the likableness would most likely have been everything you could have hoped for. Today the company may be larger, but that only means there are many more "Justins" around. The company would never have it any other way.

3

The Ladies

Shirley Durgin worked as a sales clerk in the Ladies Department for several years and occasionally filled in on the phones taking orders. She recalls one Sunday when she received a call from a gentleman in Ohio, and when she asked him if she could be of help, he replied, "If you're a widow and fifty-five, you can."

That's about what Shirley was—a widow and fifty-five—and she laughed and said so.

Well, that started it, and thereafter, whenever the man called Bean's he asked for Shirley. Even her boss, Hazel Bean, got carried away with it and would call the man about an order or something and put Shirley on the phone.

It reached the point where the man was going to drive over from Ohio and visit Shirley in Freeport, and, as Shirley tells it, she had the dickens of a time talking him out of it and winding down the telephone "affair." Just how she finally managed it, she'd never say, but those of us who knew about the situation had hoped she'd let the man come East so we could all get a good look at him. There were a few more mid-fifties widows around the place.

Mary Hawkes was with us for forty years. "I guess in about every department, except Bookkeeping," as she puts it. It still embarrasses her to this day that she was responsible for some national publicity about the company. Bean's had various form-cards for situations or questions that might arise, and on this particular occasion she hurriedly grabbed the wrong card and sent it off to a would-be customer. The recipient lived in New Mexico and Mary had mailed him a "No Foreign Shipment" card in response to an order.

That little mistake made the Associated Press news wires and everybody in the United States read about it. Dozens of letters arrived at the company, commenting on the story, and she was sure she'd be fired.

Not a chance.

"L. L. Bean," she wrote me recently, "got a kick out of the whole episode and loved all the letters and comments."

That was L. L. at his best—but then he was usually at his best.

Justin Williams, whom we heard from in the last chapter, worked for Bean's about as long as anyone and reports that he received literally thousands of comments from customers about the "wonderful" work done by the telephone operators and clerks. "Customers have the same opinion of these employees as they do of the store," he says, "and how our people manage to get along so well in the hectic atmosphere of the retail store is miraculous." Justin spent at least eight years "at the door"—sort of an unofficial troubleshooter and complaint-taker—and in that time, he says, "I can possibly think of six times a customer came out dissatisfied with a clerk. And, even then, when I'd track it down, it was usually that the clerk had spent what seemed to the customer to be too much time trying to find an article, or maybe the clerk had gone higher up for advice."

Even when things were destined to go wrong, Bean's usually caught it in the nick of time. Barbara Pohle, a telephone operator and customer-information researcher, tells this story:

Barbara: I hadn't worked at L. L. Bean's very long when this particular customer came on the line. We did not have computers to record the information as we do now. All orders were handwritten, and you had to write fast and know your merchandise. This customer had a complicated order involving several items she was sending to another person. In the midst of ordering, she asked for a gift card to be enclosed reading: "To the very best assistant ever." I picked up a gift card, and to get the information down while she was talking I abbreviated the message to read: "To the very best ass. ever." All orders were screened by our Sort Department—thank heavens!—and when Ruthie Turner spotted my card it just about made her day!

Everything the employees did in the early days was done the hard way—by hand. I joined the company in 1935 (for eighteen cents an hour, a fair wage for a beginner in those days), and it is impossible to accurately describe the immense changes that have occurred since then in respect to work requirements. I remember one of our clerks coming up the stairs one day with an armful of pants, shirts and other items representing the day's clothing orders. Today, it would take several semitrailers to hold a day's worth of such orders—up to 120,000 packages—to say nothing of the computers and automated machinery needed to handle, service and keep track of such a vast amount of goods.

But, in those days, it was just typewriters and plug-in switchboards and fans for cooling. Accounts, orders and records were entered with a typewriter or pen and ink. The inventory could be memorized in a few hours. Cutting, stitching, assembling and a host of other jobs were all done by hand. It was the Dark Ages compared to modern techniques, but the women loved it, many of them having come straight off the local farms, and

*Dot Marston (with
corsage).*

they adapted to it and enjoyed themselves and considered themselves a
family—with family loyalties. From the hearts and minds of these women at
L. L. Bean's sprang the warmth and pleasantries and helpful, concerned
responses that our many customers have come to take for granted. As one
customer described it, "Calling L. L. Bean's is like calling home and talking
to your family. There's no doubt they're glad you called, and there's no
doubt they'll do everything they can for you."

Another thing we can thank the women for was the introduction of ladies' items. It was a man's world in those early days, you know, and every now and then the girls would nudge L. L. about it and suggest he stock a few items for them. The suggestions apparently took hold, because one day Jack Gorman arranged to get 200 pairs of Bermuda shorts from Portland. (Jack managed our apparel line and he was the father of Leon Gorman, our current president.) He and I set up a table at the base of the stairs in the old store. Red, white and blue Bermudas. In a couple of days, we only had four pairs left—and L. L. was as pleased as he could be. From then on, ladies' clothes were a staple, and today they account for a third of Bean's business.

We girls know a thing or two ourselves, you know.

Dot Marston worked at L. L. Bean's for over fifty years, for most of that time as a sort of old-fashioned paymaster, but she also filled in at other jobs when the need demanded it. In this interview, she not only recalls various aspects of the inner workings of the company in former years, but pays tribute to L. L. Bean's personal generosity and concern for his employees— traits which were most unusual among business executives a few decades ago and which helped engender the loyalties of those he employed.

Dot: I can't remember exactly, but profit sharing with the employees began in either the late forties or early fifties. It was quite a new thing, and not too many people knew how it worked. In our case, the directors and accountants would figure out the money they had to work with at the end of the year and they'd put a percentage, or maybe the whole amount, into profit sharing. This money went to the eligible employees according to their basic pay and the number of years they'd worked for the company. It always had to be figured out individually.

Me: There was also *extra* money for the employees at the time of the bonus.

Dot: Oh, yes.

Me: Do you remember the year we got a really big surprise bonus? I think they paid us in installments.

Dot: Sure. They paid us so much the first week, then more the next week, and so on. They couldn't pay it all at once, you know. They paid it when they knew some money was coming in. And they wanted to keep the whole idea secret . . . a surprise. *They* couldn't plan on it until they knew the money was coming in, and they didn't want *us* to plan on it and then be disappointed.

Me: Boy! Do I remember that bonus! I will never forget it. And how they ever kept it a secret, I'll never know. We were in another world! One of the helpful things was that Bean's was a privately owned company. They didn't have to pay stockholders. This gave them a fund of money to work with that wouldn't have been available if they had been owned publicly.

Dot: That's right. Just the family. But, of course, they didn't have to give the employees a dime in bonuses. And the money for the business went fast, beyond L. L.'s expectations. He didn't want bonuses to get out of hand . . . but he gave us as much as he could and still be responsible to the business. If the company made it, we made it, and we all knew it and loved him for it.

Me: And all the figuring and everything was done manually.

Dot: Oh, yes. You remember, Carlene, we used to be paid in cash . . . you got your pay in a little brown envelope with your hours and everything figured out on the back. But that wasn't the hardest job. The really grueling job was working on the mailing lists. Here is where the term "faithful employees" took on real meaning. I remember Sylvia Estabrook would sit down and type endless sheets of addresses, correcting them, entering new ones, deleting old ones. Hour after hour after hour. She'd never complain, and she was accurate. And in the fall, when the orders were the heaviest, you could always count on the women coming in and working straight through. Talk about being faithful! Except for typing, everything was manual, although I guess you could say typing was manual by today's standards.

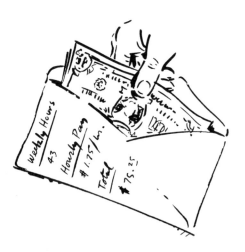

The thing is, L. L. could always count on the work being done. He didn't have to worry about it. And, of course, those addresses and orders were the heart of his business.

Me: And for laughs, when we needed a break, remember how we'd go downstairs to where they made the boot grease? And stay by the fire and label the cans?

Dot: Oh, yes. That was fun. I liked going down there.

Me: We raised holy hell down there!

Dot: I remember that three or four of us would usually go down, and they had this big tub of grease that was melted, and it had a spout or something so you could pour it into the cans. And this big wood fire was always going. We'd go down there to fill the cans and get warm.

Me: And to have a good time!

Dot: Were you with me—it was a really cold day—and Keiver Johnson put on some more wood. Well, the grease spilled over and it was an awful mess. I mean, it was all over the floor! And I told him to blame it on me.

Me: How in the world did they clean it up?

Dot: I don't know—unless they waited for the frost and then scraped it up.

Me: Will you ever forget how we used to do the catalog? Ethel Williams would take it down to the presses a couple of sheets at a time after L. L. okayed it. We used to do the whole thing on a couple of desks. Today, there's this huge room with a million easels, and they have consultations with dozens of people and it's all so high-tech.

Dot: Sure. Ethel was L. L.'s regular secretary, and once in a while, when she was busy somewhere else, like on the catalog, L. L. would ask me to take dictation. L. L. wasn't so good on grammar and I was never sure how much to change it. The way he said things was the way he wanted it written, but I'd clean it up a little bit here and there. I thought it would reflect on him better if I changed it.

Me: He probably didn't care, anyway.

Dot: Yes, but I did. I wanted people to think highly of him. Of course, he never bothered with that sort of thing. When he had something to say, he'd just say it. And usually real loud! I remember one of our employees sauntered up to me one day—I won't use his name—and said he had to talk to L. L. And I said, "Well, L. L. has been kind of curtailing callers because he hasn't been feeling too well." And this man said, "Well, he'll see me anyway." So I told him I'd go and see. I was as nice as I could be. You can never be too nice. Anyway, I went into L. L.'s office and told him about his visitor. L. L. shouted, "Don't want to hear about it! Don't want to see anybody! Nobody at all!" You could hear that booming voice of his out on the street. When I came out of the office, everybody was looking at me, asking me what I was going to tell this man. And I said, "I don't have to tell him anything. L. L.'s already told him!"

Me: L. L. put in a hospital plan for his employees back in those days.

Dot: It was 1940, I think. Years before most other companies. And then there was the Christmas cash, too. Let's not forget that! Now, this was in addition to the profit sharing and annual bonus. I tell you, you wonder why people wanted to work for L. L. and you don't have far to look.

Me: It strikes me that a lot of the work created in your department was the direct result of all the various services provided for the employees by the company. It seemed the company created a lot of the work itself because of its own generosity. And in that, I think they were way ahead of their time.

Dot: You know, it was funny. The last day I worked, I wrote a little note to Leon Gorman. I said, "Probably you know by now that I'm retiring today." And I wrote a few words about L. L. and how pleased I was personally about Leon's wanting to carry on the business. So, he said he wanted to see me before the day was through. And, you know, I think he was somewhat at a loss for words. He seemed sad. It was very personal. Very genuine. It was not a facade. He really cared and it came through. It was a nice talk. It made the many years worth it.

Me: It amazes me that, no matter how large the company becomes, there is still the completely personal touch that Leon has with the people who work here.

Dot: You see, a lot of companies have tried to mimic L. L. Bean's. I mean their policies and personnel and all, but they just can't do it.

Me: The thing that separates L. L. Bean's from other large companies is that they *genuinely* care about the people who work here—not about them as "workers" en masse, but about them as individuals. And I think that probably makes the difference in how the employees feel about themselves. It causes them to really care about representing L. L. Bean's properly—they want to put their best foot forward. Believe me, this comes across to the customers, and it is this that makes the customers love L. L. Bean's. I have never met anyone—either in catalog sales or in the showroom—who wasn't totally helpful, bending over backward to do everything I might possibly want, giving me all sorts of information.

Dot: It's the feeling the employees give the customer.

Me: And the feeling is: I'm proud to be here and I'm happy to help you. And you don't get that in most retail stores unless there is a caring from management for each individual employee.

Dot: Yes, it has to come down all the way through. And I've always felt that if I had to do it all over again, I would sign on with Bean's in an instant.

One of the executives at Bean's summed up the company's philosophy on the subject this way: "Our motto is to do unto our employees as we would have them do unto our customers."

This attitude began with L. L. Bean himself, and it has been adhered to in every way under Leon Gorman. This chapter is indeed about the loyalties and personalities of the ladies who have played such a large role in giving the company its legendary family feeling so welcomed by customers. But any one of us would be the first to assure you that Bean's management has earned everything we've given.

4

What Depression?

*I*t is an old joke in these parts that when people ask a Mainer how he fared in the Depression, the Mainer thinks for a moment about a lifetime of hard work and precious little money and answers: "What Depression?"

There is some truth to the joke, but the Depression was extra hard on the fragile economy and citizens of this state, and many a Maine company had vanished forever by the time it was over. This was not the case with L. L. Bean, Inc.—it was precisely the opposite. The company grew phenomenally, and to give you insight into the reasons for this growth in such difficult times it is necessary to introduce you—really introduce you—to L. L. Bean himself. The reputation of this man, coupled with the functional, no-frills line of goods he carried, transcended the state of the economy; people everywhere found the money to purchase his products. In many ways, L. L. Bean's was a business designed to fare well in hard times—when money could not be spent foolishly.

And as for those hard times, many of us remember them very well indeed. We remember L. L. hiring whole families—the father, the mother, the children—to help keep the little town of Freeport employed. He'd buy worms from the local kids for a penny apiece, worms he never used. The kids would come in with a can full of worms, walk right into his office, and he'd set aside whatever he was doing and take care of this important "transaction" with the kids. When people came through town looking for jobs, and if L. L. didn't have anything for them, he'd very often give them some money. Many times, he'd have an assistant call up Mary and Jack Collins' restaurant, describe the person to them, and then send him over for a free meal. Countless times, when he was off fishing somewhere, he ran into boys using make-shift rods and reels to catch something for the family's table, and he'd give them a gift of proper gear.

Yes, we remember those things . . . and Freeport remembers them. L. L. played a large role in keeping Freeport alive in the Depression, but that wasn't what brought his company through and made it prosperous. No, as I said, that was based upon the reputation of the man and his company.

Imagine, if you will, an out-of-state hunter calling L. L. Bean's, asking for L. L. personally and getting him on the phone.

L. L.: What can I do for you?

Hunter: I want to know how to find deer in the Maine woods.

L. L.: And just where in this state will you be hunting?

Hunter: Oh, up in the north somewhere, in the heavy woods.

L. L.: Look for an active cutting area. The deer will follow the loggers. They eat off the tops of the stumps.

That's the sort of practical, no-nonsense advice L. L. would give callers by the hundreds. L. L. had spent his life in the woods, as boy and man, hunted and fished every chance he had, and spoke a terse, direct-to-the-point language more akin to that of game wardens and guides than a businessman with products to sell. His tone and personality dominated his catalogs, which he edited himself. There was nothing in them that wouldn't improve a customer's hunting, fishing or camping trip . . . nothing that wasn't 100% useful, free of unnecessary frills . . . nothing that wouldn't work as he stated it would work . . . nothing that wasn't of the best quality possible . . . nothing that was overpriced . . . and nothing that wasn't guaranteed to be exactly as advertised. It was L. L. who told his customers that it was foolish to buy another pair of his Maine Hunting Shoes when the company's inexpensive repair job would make the old ones as good as new.

Consider this item from Bean's catalog in the fall of 1934. It's not just the knife that's being sold; it's the honesty, know-how and practicality of an experienced fisherman that is firmly on display. Read this, then ask yourself if you would even consider buying any other trout knife:

Bean's Trout Knife

For some time we have been perfecting a knife for cleaning game fish. This is the result.

The cutting blade is 4½" long and extends full length of large walnut handle fastened with 3 brass rivets as shown. The handle is so long (4⅝") that the hand does not come in contact with the fish. Once used you will never again use a jackknife that is more work to clean than the fish. It is a very handy knife for general camp and home use. If kept in the genuine elk leather case as shown, which completely covers knife, you will always have a clean sharp knife. Given free with $20.00 order. Price 75¢ postpaid.

L. L. wrote advertising copy like that for almost all of his products. It's different, isn't it? You believe what it says.

And well you might, because L. L. and his staff would *use* the products advertised in the catalogs. They'd try them out, put them to the test. There was no way L. L. would send someone into the woods with equipment that hadn't proved, to his personal satisfaction, to be the most useful, hardiest and most economical of its kind. It was a rare product that passed his evaluation, and when he found one he'd say so, right in the catalog, and he staked his name on it. Justin Williams recalls the time L. L. was shown a fancy new fishing rod by a salesman. The manufacturer had spent a considerable amount seeing to it that this was the best rod that could be made. The salesman really pushed it, and some other merchants had bought quite a quantity of them. "Not L. L.," said Justin. "He took the rod on a fishing trip, hooked onto a big fish, the rod snapped in half and went overboard. That was the end of that. It wasn't easy to sell something to L. L. He had to see the truth of things for himself. If he put a product in his catalog, you can bet it was tested and it was worth having, and no doubt about it at all. He started building a reputation for that right from the beginning."

By the early thirties, thanks to L. L.'s distinctive style of writing catalog copy and offering products that worked as he said they would, his reputation had spread far beyond Freeport. Hunters and fishermen felt comfortable with his catalog; they liked the way he said things and related to its woodsman's brand of integrity and common sense. Whether they planned to hunt or fish in Maine or somewhere else was of little consequence; here were the products they needed, sold by a man who understood them and whom it appeared obvious they could trust. He was one of them—and that was the key to it all. L. L. was not a merchant as such—not to the readers of his catalogs. He was a knowledgeable hunter and fisherman who knew what he was talking about. And he told them they could have their money back if they discovered otherwise.

The catalog on press, 1961.

It got to the point in the thirties where L. L.'s advice and expertise were trusted so much that hundreds of catalog readers were phoning in, insisting on talking with him personally. He had suggested in his catalog that readers were welcome to call the store for advice, but he could not have imagined how many of them wouldn't hang up until they had reached L. L. himself. When I think of L. L., I'm likely to picture him with a telephone receiver in his hand; he spent as much time on the phone as he did on other matters. Many of these calls were by no means local. His Fall catalog contained fifty-two pages in 1934, requiring twenty tons of paper, and customers could be found in nearly every nation on earth. People from places as far apart as Hudson's Bay and Brazil, California and India, would telephone him for advice, asking how to outfit a hunting or fishing party, for instance, or requesting information on the best game areas for a coming trip to Maine. Sometimes, the callers would give L. L. an outline of where they were going and confidently rely on him to select the necessary items and ship them off. Worldwide Depression or no worldwide Depression, men would hunt and fish and go into the woods as they had always done, and it seemed at times that few of them would do so without first talking with L. L. Bean.

Other markets were starting to develop for Bean's, vast markets composed of farmers and construction crews and other outdoor workers for whom L. L. Bean's tough, functional shoes, clothing and other goods were ideally suited, and these prospective customers were beginning to hear about Bean's catalog and were writing in for copies. Family camping and hiking was only beginning to come into vogue, but it represented an increasing part of the business, as did women's needs, and these, too, were addressed as the thirties wore on. If one were to obtain the best and most useful outdoor products available for one's dearly earned money in those days, one need only turn to a Bean's catalog. It wasn't the biggest catalog in the business (there was giant Sears Roebuck, remember, and several others), but there was no denying the appeal of the distinctive honesty, experienced know-how and sense of security offered up by L. L. Bean in his catalog literature. On that score, the catalog had no competition, and there was literally no containing the business that poured into the company.

Five times in the thirties, additions were made to the company's building to accommodate expanding business—in 1934, 1935, 1936, 1937 and 1939. The company was incorporated in 1934, with all but ten shares held by the family . . . twenty-four-hour retail service was instituted . . . sales passed the million-dollar mark in 1937 . . . and by the end of the decade there were nearly 200,000 names on Bean's mailing list, requiring the use of 700 tons of paper for the year's catalogs. And this was the *Depression*.

Freeport not only kept its citizens employed during those hard years, thanks in considerable measure to L. L. Bean's, but reduced its debt and increased its valuation by $100,000, an astonishing sum under the prevailing conditions. The *Portland Evening Press*, in its issue of July 1, 1939, had this to say about the town:

> Few towns in the state have a more enviable record of employment than this thriving village, known far and wide as the home of the L. L. Bean Company, Inc. and also as the birthplace of Maine. With numerous other towns and cities depending upon Federal aid projects to provide employment, the town of Freeport points to as many as 1,450 persons employed in peak seasons and approximately 850 on the payroll at all times.

Earlier in the decade, the *Brunswick Record* took note of the company's fast growth and also included a few personal glimpses of its founder. The following is excerpted from an article in its edition of August 23, 1934:

> In the space of 20 years, L. L. Bean of Freeport has seen his business rise from a new shoe that he designed and had made for his personal

use to a tremendous mail-order house whose catalogs go to every nation on earth. . . . L. L. Bean, himself, is as interesting a man as his business. He would like to fish at Sebago in preference to meeting the King of England. He packs up his car every year to go after a deer. And these trips are not only for recreation, for he tests out new devices that he plans to catalog next year. This testing-out may be a secret of the popularity of his goods. If L. L. says a new coat is good, it's because he wore it on a moose-hunting trip . . . L. L. Bean remains a small-town businessman. He likes Freeport, and knows everyone by his or her first name . . . A Maharaja of India buys Bean's goods and outfits for his entire retinue. Babe Ruth, Jack Holt, Squire Sharkey, and all such folks are regular customers. Mr. Bean has a nice thank-you letter from President Roosevelt, praising the quality of an article in the Bean line . . ."

And, finally, this one sentence from the same article, which pleases me greatly: "And to Mr. Bean's credit it must be said that his employees are well paid; his help are all rooters for his business."

You bet we were. I was there, and I know.

How could we be otherwise?

My most distinct memories of the Depression are of my fellow employees at Bean's. To work for that company at that time, with its growth and activity, was a privilege beyond anything you can imagine. The job was secure, the working conditions and benefits were glorious for the era, and one had the distinct feeling that he or she was part of a family with the most tolerant and compassionate of patriarchs. Everyone in America worked hard for every dime they earned in those days, and we at Bean's worked as hard as any of them to keep what we had. There was no such thing then of having just one job. When help was needed in another department, we gave it, if we knew how. There was no caste system or preciousness about anything;

what needed to be done was done by the first free hand available. We'd type, cut, sew, wait on customers, operate the switchboard, work on the mailing lists, sweep the place out, greet customers at the door—whatever was necessary to keep the "family house" operating and in order. Above all was our determination to support L. L., maintain the quality of the products and never be responsible for the loss of a customer. L. L.'s personality and expertise brought the customer in, either personally or through the catalog, and it was up to us to satisfy and keep that customer. This we did. And when someone would send in a pair of ten-year-old Maine Hunting Shoes that had obviously seen extremely heavy-duty use—and the owner insisted they hadn't lived up to their advertising—we'd put on new soles, or whatever was required, and ship them back with a "Thank You" note. Likely as not—and this happened again and again—the owner would eventually send in orders for other items that more than made up for the cost of the initial shoe repairs. And that brings up an important point:

Probably every new employee of Bean's—familiar with the less-than-honest ways of much of the world—has questioned the wisdom of Bean's legendary 100% guarantee. But mighty few of them, if they looked at the records, could long doubt its value. We've been "stuck" many times through no fault of our products, but that guarantee is cast in stone and it has won this company infinite goodwill and subsequent business that far outshadows any losses incurred by fulfilling it. Imagine, if you will, a fellow who is sure he "put something over" on us, displaying his freely repaired boots to his friends. No matter what he says, somebody in that room will be impressed by the integrity and decency of our company. That's what will register, and right there L. L. Bean's has the makings of a new customer, and maybe a roomful of them.

Earlier in this chapter I referred to the sense of "family" we had at Bean's. It may sound like a cliché to some of you, but it was very real. It had

The original White sewing machine used by Kippy Goldrup's mother, Gertrude Goldrup, is now on display at Bean's.

nothing to do with the cozier size of the company in the thirties; it sprang from the way the business was managed. In the most difficult economic times this nation has ever faced, decent human values were never compromised at Bean's. In one form or another, management shared its earnings with its employees. Our jobs would not be lost, except for very good reason. Products weren't subtly cheapened to build sales (which would have just as subtly undermined the pride and spirit of Bean's craftspeople). The Bean guarantee remained in full force despite the public's obvious need to take advantage of every opportunity to conserve money. I could give further examples, but let me sum it up this way: Not in the more than forty-five years I've been with Bean's has this company ever had more reason to lower both its human and product standards than it had in the Depression, but not once in those many years have I ever seen it happen.

A company like that becomes a "family" . . . a "family" we're proud of and spontaneously give our best for . . . and this has almost invariably become the case with Bean's employees once they become fully aware of just what it is that makes up this company's character.

Like L. L.'s catalog . . . you can trust it.

5

*The Famous
and Not-So-Famous*

Many famous people can be counted among L. L. Bean's customers, ranging from U.S. presidents and foreign royalty to some of the best-known names in sports and show business. It is always interesting to see celebrities in the retail store, and there is often some aspect of these visits that is remembered long after the personage has left. Not so long ago, for example, one of the most talented of all country and pop singers, John Denver, was examining selections at the store's knife counter. Nearby, Lawrence Worden, one of our sales reps, was helping an older couple try on some shoes; the woman leaned over to her husband and whispered, "Look! There's John Denver!" Whereupon the husband said, in a voice loud enough to be heard very clearly at the knife counter, "Who the hell is John Denver?"

So much has been written about our celebrated visitors in the company's

Margaret Chase Smith and me during our interview. (Courtesy Andrew Freemire)

newsletters and in articles and books about the company that I hesitate to go over the same ground. Here and there, however, in my research and interviewing, I did manage to root out some original anecdotes or gather insights and fresh viewpoints from the elite and illustrious personalities who have visited our store.

Margaret Chase Smith, for instance, perhaps the most revered of Maine's U.S. senators, visited Bean's on several occasions and was certainly one of our more delightful customers. In an interview with me a few years ago, she recalls one of these visits and gives us a keen look into the personality and special kind of thoughtfulness that so endeared her to Mainers:

Smith: I don't think I met L. L. Bean more than a couple of times, and it was probably when I was campaigning for office. I'd always pay my respects to the head of a place where I was campaigning—in this case Mr. Bean's retail store—and I'd ask if it would be all right for me to go through. There's a difference among politicans, you know. Some of them only go into places like this at election time. And they just go in, shake hands with all of the help, and this is a nuisance. It interrupts and interferes with the work and is a disservice. I didn't do it that way. I would go in and go to the office and ask for permission. I wouldn't have campaigned at L. L. Bean's if I hadn't had permission, you may be sure of that.

Senator Smith didn't have to ask permission. L. L. would have been honored to have her walk through the store. But she didn't take it for granted any more than she took the citizens of Maine for granted.

Senator Smith recalled another incident that illustrated not only her respect for Maine's citizens, but also her savviness in dealing with Congress. This particular vignette has nothing to do with Bean's directly, but it deserves to be recorded in the annals of effective, Downeast politicking. The story concerns the dredging of one of our local harbors:

Smith: They wanted some dredging done because the fishermen were having a hard time with the shallows. I went to work on it. Some of the town—I won't try to identify them—was against it. They said all I was doing was catering to the yachtsmen—that I was trying to get it dredged so that the summer people—the city people—could come in and use those ports. And I said, "No, it's the fishermen." So I called a couple of the fishermen late in the afternoon one day and I said, "I have this project through for you, but I'm afraid I'm going to lose it unless some of you come down here (to Washington) and prove a point for me." So they got themselves dressed up, caught a late evening plane, and they walked into my office at 9 A.M. the following morning. The chairman of the particular committee we had to face that day was from Louisiana, and he said, "Now, Margaret, you can have five minutes. That's all you can have." And I said, "Okay, I have my people coming all the way from Maine." And he said, "Remember, that's all we have, Margaret. Five minutes. We have a lot going on this morning." So, those two fishermen—real, honest-to-goodness Atlantic fishermen—with brown, burned hands and weathered skin, all dressed up in their best suits, sat down at the table. They had brought with them a little model of a lobster trap and they put it up on the table. There were about four or five on that committee, and, of course, they were all eyes. And do you know that those fishermen started talking, and they went on for one solid hour! The committee members kept asking them questions, and those fishermen explained how the lobster traps worked, how they caught the lobsters, how they threw them back if they weren't of proper length . . . and they answered anything and everything the committee members wanted to know. It was a real education. And I got my money for the dredging! I couldn't have done it without those fishermen and their straight, honest talk—something you don't get too often in Washington, but something you find a lot of in the average American. They just need to be heard.

At one point in my conversation with Senator Smith, we realized we had some mutual friends in Freeport and a number of other things in common, except that she had gone to the Senate while I had gone to L. L. Bean's. She graciously replied: "I didn't have enough sense to work for L. L. Bean."

Maine was blessed to have someone as sensitive and decent as that in Washington.

Eleanor Roosevelt visited the retail store on several occasions and, for some reason, most of these visits provided grist for anecdotes. Either she wasn't recognized, or employees fell over themselves to be of help or she'd stumble into an odd situation, and so on. One of the funniest anecdotes concerns Mrs. Roosevelt and L. L. Bean, himself, and even if some of you may have heard it, it's worth repeating.

I'm not sure exactly who told me this, but whoever it was had been cleaning up in the stitching room at the store and was in a line-of-sight position to witness the unfolding events. Mrs. Roosevelt was in town on this occasion, and word had gone out that she was to visit the store. It was about the time of day when L. L. usually went home, but he was excited about meeting Mrs. Roosevelt, so he stayed in his office. He didn't want Mrs. Roosevelt to think he'd been waiting for her, so when he heard footsteps coming up the stairs, he picked up the phone and pretended to be talking business. His phone, however, was one of the new ones at the time and he wasn't used to it. It had a French receiver and he had put the wrong end to his ear. He apparently realized it as his illustrious visitor came through the door and, according to our witness, he was "all shook up." Anyway, he greeted Mrs. Roosevelt.

Only it wasn't Mrs. Roosevelt. It was Mrs. Winslow, the cleaning lady. For a few startling moments, she was greeted like royalty. L. L. didn't have a clue as to what Mrs. Roosevelt looked like, of course, and Mrs. Winslow had all she could do to get a word in edgewise and identify herself.

"So here was L. L.," relates our witness, "summoning up his most proper and formal behavior to welcome the First Lady of the land. As for me, watching all this, I had to grip one of the stitching machines with both hands to keep from collapsing on the floor in laughter."

To list the celebrities who have filed through Bean's store would take

Leon Gorman and CBS newscaster, Dan Rather.

Frequent customer,
Babe Ruth, 1934.

many, many pages, to say nothing of listing those who order from the catalog. Relatively recent visitors have included such notables as Richard and Pat Nixon, Dan Rather, Ted Williams and the immensely popular weatherman and raconteur of NBC's *Today Show*, Willard Scott. Willard is a frequent visitor to the store, and, as many viewers of the *Today Show* know, he is continually being kidded about his hairpiece. On one of his visits to the store he was trying on sweaters, and, sure enough, his hairpiece came off in the process. It didn't bother Willard a bit and the onlookers, of course, were in raptures.

Boston Red Sox great,
Ted Williams and me.
(Courtesy Andrew
Freemire)

Boston Red Sox great Ted Williams is a long-time Bean's customer. His feats on the playing field are unmatched, and so are the feet on his legs— they're more than a half-size in difference. "If I buy a pair of shoes in a twelve," he says, "my right foot just slops in it. If I get an eleven, it's a little too tight on my right foot. So, I always get a twelve for my left foot and an eleven-and-a-half for my right foot, and I've never had any trouble about it at Bean's. I've always liked Bean's. They've been great to me."

Our pleasure, Ted.

It's in the day-to-day dealing with our thousands of average, noncelebrity customers, however, that the special spirit of Bean's is most often on display.

For example, Ed Dwyer, who worked for us in Personnel and in the retail store until 1985, tells this little story:

Ed: While serving as a sales rep in the retail store, I sold a camping stove to a lady who was going to tour Ireland. She had no sooner left the store than I realized she could have difficulty locating the proper fuel in Ireland. I was concerned about this and went to the cashier and found that she had paid with a check that listed a town in Vermont as the only address. The next day, with a more appropriate backpacking stove in hand (it was my day off, Sunday) I drove to the small town in Vermont, went up to the general store and was given directions to the customer's house. I found the woman, exchanged stoves, and instructed her in how to use it. It was a beautiful Sunday trek for me—and the postcards I received from Ireland confirmed the fact that L. L. Bean had another satisfied customer.

I'll bet she was satisfied.

Same for the customer who walked into L. L.'s office one day wearing a different shoe on each foot. She just barged right in and asked L. L. which shoe suited her the best. L. L. stopped what he was doing, looked the shoes over and gave her his decision. The woman was delighted.

Several of the respondents to my questionnaire report that they've made lifelong friends with customers they've met while working at Bean's. It's not unusual for our employees to receive occasional "thank you" letters and even gifts from customers they've helped. Expressions of customer appreciation are by no means isolated occurrences, and our "Customer Comments" cards are largely a collection of accolades for Bean's employees.

Of course, we occasionally have irascible customers who aren't delighted with anything.

Mary Dyer, who worked in several departments, tells about the customer who mailed in an order with some cash for a particular style of socks.

"He enclosed too much money for one pair," reports Mary, "but not enough for two pair. We politely wrote and asked him whether he wanted one pair or two pair. His reply was as follows: 'I only need one pair! What the hell would I do with two pair of socks!' We sent his order off and just as politely thanked him for it.

"On another occasion," says Mary, "a man planning a fishing trip ordered some live worms listed in our catalog. We don't sell them any more, but in those days we did and we used to keep them in a refrigerator in the basement. In due time, the worms were returned to us with a full-page, single-spaced, typewritten letter of explanation. Part of the letter, with the misspelling of 'worms,' reads as follows: 'Any fool knows the difference between garden warms and dung warms! Dung warms are *red!* Garden warms are *brown!* I ordered garden warms!!!' We refunded his money, of course, and I always wanted to send him a spelling book."

About the only time I can remember one of us skirting around the edges of impoliteness to a customer was when Ruthie Turner was taking her very last telephone order at the end of a long, complicated shift. She was one of only two or three overwhelmed order-takers that day, and the man on the phone was a real conversationalist about everything except the order he'd called about. "Are you really in Maine?" asked the caller, in the midst of one of his ramblings. "I can't believe I'm actually talking with someone in Maine. And at L. L. Bean!"

"Yes you are, sir," said Ruthie, finally reaching the end of her rope, "and if you'll just let me get this chicken off my desk, I'll take your order."

Now, that's not so bad.

In fact, I think it's sort of like L. L.'s terse comment to hunters who wonder how many to take on a hunting party—six, eight, ten, twelve?

"Two is a good number," advises L. L. flatly. "That is, if you plan to hunt."

Perhaps the most accommodating we have ever been to a customer occurred when a New York couple arrived at the store, did their shopping and then asked how far North they'd have to drive to see some moose.

Cover of the 1928 fall catalog.

Now, it so happened that for the only time in anyone's memory, and perhaps for all time to come, there were three moose at that very moment in the neighbor's garden that backed up to the side of the store in those days. "Just step right over here to the window," said the clerk, "and you'll see just what you're looking for. No need to drive an inch. Bean's provides everything."

That story, now that I think of it, however, vies with another one for customer-accommodation honors. It happened during the worst days of the Depression:

A local youngster—about ten or so—started coming into the store every day just before closing time. He was saving up for a particular fishing rod, and every day he came by to be sure that rod was still in the display rack. He could only earn pennies at a time, doing odd jobs after school, and he'd count his day's earnings in front of the counter and figure out how much more he needed.

It was a slow, discouraging process, and it went on for weeks, day after day, until it finally reached the ears of L. L.—who saw to it that he was at the counter the next time the lad came in.

In walked the boy the next day, right on schedule, going up to the rod rack and inspecting his longed-for treasure from top to bottom. . . . then out came the pennies he'd earned that day (twelve cents on this particular day) and up walked L. L. . . .

"I hear you've been saving up for this rod, son. Well, I'm the owner of this store, and I think you've saved just about the right amount. I'll take this rod out of the rack right now and give it to the salesman here, and you come back tomorrow with the money you've saved and he'll give you the rod and some line and flies to go with it."

It is my conviction that never has there been a happier customer of Bean's than that youngster.

One of the most unusual tributes to the company's concern and care for customers was penned by a New Mexico woman, Peggy Bond Church. Ms. Church was still using Bean's products at the age of 82, and, in 1986, New Mexico named her an official "Living Treasure." Her tribute to Bean's was a bit of poetry, and it was published in *The Atlantic*, July, 1949:

My prophet for this modern scene
is L. L. Bean
who through life's woods in sun or snow
will outfit me to go
in featherweight attire most safely pent
from any element.

I wear Bean's shoes upon my feet,
both waterproof and neat.
I carry all my comforts at my back
in Bean's approved pack,
and bed myself upon, when I'm all in,
Bean's rubber tarpaulin.

Armed with Bean's axe, whose most commended grace
is to reflect my face,
dangling Bean's feathered minnow in my hand,
serene I stand
in this confused world, equipped with lure
infallible and sure.

Naught shall affright me. Have I not Bean's word
through all dilemmas heard?
Though lost in wilderness my wild surmise
is that Bean's compass lies
I'll not despair. The obvious thing to do,
says Bean, is carry two!

The inspiration for the last verse of Ms. Church's poem could only have come from one of the compass advertisements in the L. L. Bean catalogs. Here's one from the fall 1937 edition:

Bean's Maine Woods Compass

Actual Size $2.85

$3.15

After looking over dozens of compasses of different makes we picked the Hunter Case as being the most practical style but it had the same fault of all high grade compasses. The dial was all cluttered up with figures, lines and ornaments.

We, therefore, had a very plain dial made to our own idea as shown. At a glance you can see the four points of compass even on a very dark day. We also had an arrow needle so that there is no question which end points North.

These Compasses are made for us by the most reliable company we know of.

The needle is jewelled and balanced to offset dip.

Two styles: one plain White-Metal as shown at left and one Gold-Bronze with fancy edge and Butler graining top and bottom as shown at right. The Gold-Bronze case is fast color and a little larger. It is a very handsome compass.

When closed needle is automatically locked to avoid unnecessary wear. In fact the compass with our improved dial is the best and most sensitive of any instrument we examined regardless of price. Each Compass has chamois skin case.

Price, White-Metal Case $2.85 postpaid. Gold-Bronze Case $3.15 postpaid.

The best compass in the world is useless if you do not know how to use it. Therefore, we furnish free complete directions, "How to Use a Compass."

Oftentimes a person will believe his compass is wrong. In fact, compasses have been known to get out of order. We recommend that you carry two. I personally use our Emergency Kit Compass shown on page 4 to check by.

There is no record of L. L.'s reaction when he first read Ms. Church's poem, but my best guess is that he would have been totally speechless.

6

Smoked Sailfish and Other Tidbits

*I*n the early forties, L. L. and his wife, Claire, began spending their winters in Florida. L. L. was in his late sixties, and although he'd been slowed down somewhat by eye and ear troubles, he was otherwise more hale and hearty than most of his contemporaries—a fact which he many times attributed to his active outdoor life. In fact, in the Foreword to his autobiography, *My Life*, which he wrote in 1961, he sums it up as follows:

> The one thing I learned throughout my lifetime is the fact that outdoor recreation, such as hunting, fishing, camping and baseball games, has added years to my life span, also to the lives of my two companions. For the last sixty years, our only hobby has been outdoor recreation . . . Our ages range from 87 to 88, and all are in good physical condition and alert. We still enjoy the same sports. The other

*L. L. Bean with sailfish
caught in Florida 1941.*

members of my family, not lovers of the great outdoors, have passed
away at an early age. My Father and Mother both died, a few days
apart, at the ages of 43 and 41. These facts prove to me that outdoor
life adds years to your life.

Since the great outdoors is also a big help in keeping boys and
girls out of trouble, I wish to dedicate this book to the teenagers of
America.

When L. L. started spending his winters in Florida, he was deprived of
the deep Maine woods and northern lakes and bays, so he threw himself

wholeheartedly into deep-sea fishing. In time, it became as much a passion for him as traipsing through the snows of Maine on the trail of deer or bear, and he often sent photographs and letters back to the company full of enthusiastic accounts of his new hobby.

One spring, not long before his expected return to Maine, he forwarded up a sailfish he had caught and which he had arranged to have smoked for preservation and future good eating. The sailfish was supposed to have gone to his house in Freeport, but there was a mix-up and it was delivered to the factory and placed on L. L.'s desk in his office.

No one knows who took the first slice out of the sailfish, but seeing this beautiful smoked fish on his desk day after day was more than passersby could stand—and, slice by slice, it began to disappear. After one entire side of the fish had been eaten, somebody figured, "Hell, we've done one whole side, we might as well . . ." and so it went, until the fish had been totally devoured.

When L. L. and Claire arrived, maybe a couple of weeks later, he went looking for his smoked sailfish. People admitted it had arrived and been placed on his desk, but nobody would own up as to who had eaten it. They would say things like, "Yeah, I remember seeing it there, but, gee, beats me what could have happened to it." It was that sort of thing.

L. L. wasn't as much angry about it as he was disgusted. "Just plain disgusted," as one of his close associates put it with a twinkle in his eye (could *he* have been among the culprits?). Anyway, no one knows. Or at least, to this day, no one is telling.

L. L. wouldn't just send goodies back for himself, of course; he would also mail up all kinds of things for his poor workers toiling faithfully in sub-zero Maine. Oranges, grapefruit and other Florida specialties would arrive frequently—as would dog biscuits for Sandy, Justin Williams's big, strong, 125-pound Chesapeake Retriever. Now, herein lies a tale or two . . .

Justin: L. L. was going duck hunting with Claire one day, and he asked me to come along and bring Sandy to retrieve. Claire was scared to death of that dog, and I had second thoughts about mixing Claire and Sandy together, but I couldn't give up a good day of hunting, so I got Sandy and away we went. As it so happened, when we got to where we were going, L. L., Claire and Sandy had to get into a little pram and go out to an island. Well, I had this old Champion outboard motor that worked just fine if you knew how to work the choke, and I attached it to the pram and off they went. About three hundred feet out the motor stalled, and L. L. stood up and started pulling on the starter cord. L. L.'s pretty heavy in a boat, especially a small pram, and of course that motor wasn't about to start unless he used the choke just right. So, I'm shouting at him: "Shut the choke! Pull it out! Pull it out!" And the pram's rocking and everything as he's pulling on that cord. And just about then, L. L. made a real big mistake; he stepped on Sandy's foot! That big dog came up off the floor of the pram and just about made it over the side, knocking Claire up against the bow and coming within an inch of swamping the boat. I swore she was going into the water right then and there. I started peeling off my clothes, dead sure I'd have to swim out quick; but right then, by God, the motor started and the pram got some headway and stabilized. Sandy stayed real quiet, probably because I was in deep prayer that he wouldn't move a muscle until they all got to the island. I tell you, that was no joke. They came within a hair's breadth of going in the water that day, and it was cold and it was deep and I don't know what I could have done. All I know is I was about undressed at that point and ready to swim.

Me: Tell the rest of the story. It gets better.

Justin: Well, they get to the island, and L. L. makes his second big mistake. We had a blind all made up on the far side of the island, so that's where L. L. went with the dog, but there was no place in the blind to tie him. So, L. L. decides to tie Sandy's leash around his leg. As I said, that was his

Justin Williams and his big dog, Sandy.

second mistake. L. L. shot at a duck, and whether he got the duck or not, we'll never know, but Sandy decides he's goin'. L. L. didn't decide he was goin', but he was goin' anyway. The dog pulled him right through the side of the blind; it was totally wrecked by the time I got to it, and God knows what Claire was doing while all that was going on. We heard later she was hanging on to L. L., trying to save him. Sandy was a hound of hell to her, and she probably figured he was dragging her husband off to the nether-world or something. And you can tell this to your readers, too, although some of them won't believe it, but it's true. Not long after I got Sandy, I was in taking a bath and Sandy came in and dropped a bird in the tub with me. He'd somehow gotten it out in the yard.

During World War II, L. L. considered it his duty to serve the country, and in the earliest days of the war he was called to Washington to work with a special committee responsible for selecting and developing cold weather wearing apparel for the army. There was quite a difference of opinion on footwear, especially as to the height of the leather-topped, rubber-bottomed boots that were being considered.

Most of the committee members were quite a bit younger than L. L. and came from the West and South. They were strongly in favor of a 16-inch or even 18-inch boot, but L. L., as he writes in his autobiography, came from a colder climate:

> . . . and having tramped through the woods for many years, [I] knew from experience that a high boot would bind the leg muscles of a man who had to be on his feet all day, so that he would soon be lame and sore and unable to walk at all. I was in favor of the 10″ height I had used so much, but we finally compromised, and a 12″ boot was adopted. The result was that later we were given a large order for 12″ leather-top rubbers. These were made on the pattern of our Maine Hunting Shoe.

L. L. was a patriot and never objected to spending an inordinate amount of time in Washington during the war years where he could be of help on any number of projects—but he was also a direct, no-nonsense Mainer who knew the value of simple, practical solutions. He and those who worked for him frequently had to cut through complicated, unrealistic Washington suggestions to arrive at answers that would really work for our armed forces. One problem, for example, was to develop a quick-release method for boots used aboard ship on wet and icy decks (at times it was necessary for men to quickly remove their boots before going overboard). L. L. writes:

Many elaborate schemes were devised, but my son, Carl, came up with a very simple idea: Instead of lacing the five eyelets from the bottom up, a small loop was made in the laces and they were laced from the top eyelet down. In an emergency, a man grasped the small loop at the top and the laces came out, leaving him free to kick off the boots.

Bean's made many "navy boots" (similar to the army version), and Mary Dyer remembers lacing them in the special way devised by Carl.

World War II, of course, brought on many shortages that affected the business (it was difficult, for instance, to get enough paper for the catalog), but shortages were accepted and taken in stride while the nation's attention, including L. L. Bean's, was focused on matters other than commerce. Bean's made axes and briefcases for the armed forces, in addition to boots. But, in general, and with the exception of erecting a new building that significantly expanded floor space, the business marked time as our men and women fought against Germany and Japan.

Speaking of wartime shortages, it was particularly true in regard to machinery and hardware, to say nothing of trying to find skilled machinists and mechanics, most of whom had gone off to war. This didn't directly affect the company in any serious way, but the reliability gap in wartime civilian products did have its impact on some of L. L.'s scarce moments of leisure time—as you will see from this amusing account by George Soule:

George: L. L. decided to buy a motorboat. He'd ordered it from Massachusetts, it was about twenty feet long, and he was having it delivered to one of the launching ramps at Lake Sebago. (He had a camp on the lake.) When the boat arrived, L. L. got a bunch of us from the shop to unload it, and after we finished, L. L. sort of sidled up to me and said, "George, these other fellows are going back, but we ought to try this boat out." I said,

George Soule.

"OK." So I stayed and the rest of 'em went home. We got in the boat and went to his camp to pick up the fishing tackle, and then we started out for White's Bridge when I heard this noise. One of the spokes had fallen off the steering wheel. And I thought, "Well, that's nothing. They're just screwed on anyway." So, I reached down to pick up the spoke, and *another* one fell off. And I got that one back on, and then another one fell off. So we put *that* back together, and got everything going, and we went up through the bridge—and damned if the flywheel didn't come off the engine. Clunk. It fell right there. Well, as it happened, the wind drifted us ashore to this dock. Of course, in putting a flywheel on, you need a great big heavy wrench. The nut is like two inches across. I could put it on, but you couldn't tighten it up. So I walked up into the yard where we went ashore, and apparently a plumber lived there—I never did find out—because a piece of scrap sheet lead was lying there. Now, you could cut that with a knife; so I cut out a washer and took it down to the boat and managed to hand-tighten the nut enough so that it ate into the washer and held pretty well. We started back for the camp and got pretty close before it came off again, but we drifted in right to the camp.

Well, L. L. wasn't too happy about all of that. The product didn't stand up to what he thought it should. So he called up the engine people, and they were apologizing and they said they'd come right out and fix it, which they did, the next day, I think, and they called L. L. and said, "It's all ready to go, Mr. Bean." And L. L. says, "Well, one of you be there Thursday morning, because I'm coming up to go fishing." And the man says, "There's no need of us being there." And L. L. says, "I'd like to have one of you there to be sure it's all right." So, the man agreed, and met up with L. L. on Thursday (I didn't go), and they started out from the basin—and damned if the flywheel didn't come off again! So they got it back to the camp somehow, and the man said they would put in a brand new engine. "We'll take a day or two," the man said, "change the engine, then give you a call." So, the man called back in a couple of days and told L. L. the boat was all ready to go and it was running just fine. "Well, that's good," says L. L., "I'm going up Wednesday to try it out and there's no need for you to be there this time. I'll take your word for it." So, he went up Wednesday—and the boat was sunk at the dock.

Me: You're kidding.

George: Not a bit. It was dead sunk. The new engine didn't line up just where the old one did, so they had to bore four new holes in the hull. The trouble was they forgot to plug the old holes.

Me: Did he give them the boat back?

George: No. He kept it. Used it quite a few years. He was really tested that time, but that's an example of how unreliable things were in those days. You got what was available, and you made do with it.

The end of World War II brought a bonanza of business for the company—hundreds of thousands of service personnel were returning from the war zones intent on restructuring their lives and enjoying leisure sports and

George Soule. "Except for God," as one admirer put it, "nobody makes a duck like George Soule." (Photo courtesy Donald E. Johnson)

other recreational activities which had long been denied to them and their families. The business potential was literally unlimited, but although Bean's was well-known among sportsmen, both in America and abroad, it still needed a special boost to join the ranks of the nation's truly major mail-order businesses.

This boost was provided in December of 1946 by an article in the *Saturday Evening Post*, America's most widely read weekly magazine. The article was a long, thorough, very entertaining multipage account of L. L. Bean and his company, replete with personal insights and anecdotes that brought both the man and his company—and his products and business methods—to the attention of millions of Americans. Nineteen thousand catalog requests were generated by the article, but that was nothing compared to the lasting effects of bringing L. L. Bean's name to prominence from one coast to the other, and, indeed, around the world.

Three years later, to add icing to the publicity cake, a section about L. L. Bean appeared in Tom Mahoney's *The Great Merchants*—a major book devoted to the analysis of America's greatest retailers and their companies. L. L. thought highly enough of Mr. Mahoney's account to quote several pages of it in his autobiography, but it was the *Saturday Evening Post* article that put the Bean name into every household in America, and, in my view, this was the single most important publicity event in the company's history.

But what do I know?

One thing I can tell you, the employees were busier in the postwar years than they'd ever been before, although this didn't stop them from having fun now and then. Some of the fellows, for example, had a rifle range set up underneath the local funeral parlor and passersby could sometimes hear the firing. A co-worker of mine was on her way to lunch one day when she was stopped by a startled stranger and asked if she'd just heard shots from what seemed to be a funeral parlor across the street.

"Oh, that," she said, "they're just making sure they're dead."

7

Upstairs, Downstairs

Public television's finest hour—in the minds of many viewers—was the long-running, oft-repeated "Masterpiece Theatre" serial, *Upstairs, Downstairs*.

Set in Victorian England, the storyline revolved around the interconnected fortunes of an affluent London family (the *upstairs*) and its domestic help (the *downstairs*). As events would affect the lives of one, so, too, would they affect the lives of the other, and the matchless craft of the series lay in its portrayal of the separate views, fears and hopes the upstairs and downstairs would hold on the common matters affecting them all. If the master of the house fell seriously ill, for example, the worry and concern of both the upstairs and downstairs would be equal and evident; true affections and loyalties ran deep in this household. But the changes that might be in store should the master die—the sale of the London house, perhaps—were necessarily viewed from subtly different perspectives and with equally different personal fears and worries.

Leon Leonwood Bean died at Pompano Beach, Florida, on February 5, 1967. He was 94, and to say that this was the passing of a patriarch and considered at the time as the passing of an era, is to understate the matter considerably. L. L. *was* the company—and I know of no employee (and I wouldn't have wanted to know one) who didn't have tears in his or her eyes when the solemn news of L. L.'s death came to us. We were the downstairs of the L. L. Bean household, sharing the same sorrow as the upstairs, but the downstairs didn't share the inside information and plans of the upstairs. Some employees were unsure of what the future might have in store for the company, its ownership, its structure—and its coveted jobs.

Rumors were abundant, ranging from the certainty of the company's sale and relocation to a complete reorganization doing away with the retail store and dozens of jobs. Those of us who had been with Bean's for many years and knew the executives of the company, spent a good bit of our time knocking down such rumors and reassuring others that everything would proceed in an orderly fashion—we didn't see much chance for earth-shattering surprises. L. L. was a one-man show, no doubt about it, and he ran his business accordingly, but, in so doing, he epitomized common sense, stability and humanity, and the bulk of his directors were family, of the same stuff as L. L. Oh, there'd be some changes here and there, but nothing that would send anyone into the unemployment line; whatever changes came along would be designed to strengthen the company and the jobs of everyone in it. You'd be surprised how often some of us had to sing that song to calm the fears of newer employees.

To show you how silly it could get in the days immediately following L. L.'s passing, here's a conversation I can remember with a five-year employee, a man who should have known better. I'll call him "Mr. X." He was talking with me at the end of an easy day—a rarity—and I'm afraid I was feeling mischievous. This is pretty much how it went:

Mr. X: Jeez, Carlene, I hear they sold the company.

Me: Really? To whom?

Mr. X: Well, I don't know for sure. But maybe to Sears, Roebuck. I heard that name.

Me: Can you keep a secret? I mean a *big* secret?

Mr. X (all ears): Sure.

Me: Well, I don't want this known just yet, but I've been here over thirty years, you know, and I've saved up a whole lot of money. Hardly ever spent a dime on myself, you see. You can imagine what that adds up to in thirty years. And I've got two other girlfriends who did the same thing. Well . . . among us, and with some help from the bank, we have enough for the down payment on the company. Now, we never thought they'd go for it, of course, but they said they liked the idea of employees buying them out and they'd consider it before accepting the offer from Sears. Just this morning, they agreed to let me buy L. L. Bean's, so the news you got about Sears, you see, is old news. The real buyer is *me!*

Mr. X (absolutely stunned): Boy! That's fantastic! Congratulations! Jeez, that's terrific!

And, with that, he was off. I expected him to get that rumor started, and I was disappointed to learn that the first person he told it to was an old-timer who laughed his head off. That stopped the rumor right there.

Gee, I thought I made it sound pretty good.

Carl Bean, L. L.'s son, assumed the presidency upon his father's passing, but died an untimely death the following October. Leon A. Gorman, L. L.'s grandson, then assumed the presidency, inaugurating what one long-term employee graciously, and rightfully, came to label some years later as "The second era of L. L."

I think the best way to introduce Leon Gorman is to quote from an address he gave before The Newcomen Society in 1981. In it, he speaks about his early days at the company, his work with L. L., and shares the personal and business views he developed that eventually steered the company to success well beyond anything L. L. (or the rest of us) could have imagined back in 1967. The speech was printed by The Newcomen Society. I'm sure that some of you may have read it in other L. L. Bean literature, but I'm equally sure that many of you haven't, and excerpts from his talk require a place here before we begin looking into employee shenanigans from the late sixties to the present. Now, then, meet Leon Gorman.

The directors of L. L. Bean, Inc., not long before L. L. Bean's death in 1967. Left to right: Shailer Hayes, L. L. Bean, his sons Warren and Carl Bean, and grandsons Tom and Leon Gorman.

My fellow members of Newcomen:

In the March 1980 issue of the *TWA Ambassador* magazine Ms. Suzanne McNear wrote: "The story of L. L. Bean is an American story about a dream that did not go wrong. It is a story about honesty, reliability, promises kept, guarantees made good even after twenty or thirty years or more. It is about a one-man operation that grew, about

a family and about success—for that is certainly part of the American dream—and, finally, it is about the land and people who live close to it, or wish they did."

Many articles have been written about Leon L. Bean and his company, but Ms. McNear has summarized the theme of our history as well as any.

L. L. grew up in the hill country of Western Maine during the late 1800's. Orphaned at the age of 12, he had to make his own way working on the farms of friends and relatives. He earned a little money trapping and, in 1891, paid for two years at Kents Hill Academy by selling soap from door-to-door.

Nineteen hundred and seven found L. L. in Freeport working at his brother Ervin's haberdashery store. Among other things, they sold overalls and shirts at 39¢ each and L. L. earned $12.00 a week. He was more concerned, however, with keeping his feet dry and comfortable on deer hunting trips. The all leather loggers' boots of the day gave good support, but were heavy and wet. All rubber boots were dry, but clumsy to wear.

L. L. fashioned some lightweight leather uppers on rubber overshoe bottoms and added other refinements. He wore them afield and was delighted with the results. He made several more pairs for his hunting companions. They, too, liked the boots' dry, lightweight comfort and encouraged L. L. to sell them to the public.

In 1912 he obtained a mailing list of Maine hunting license holders, set up shop in Ervin's basement, and prepared a 3-page brochure that loudly proclaimed: "You cannot expect success hunting deer or moose if your feet are not properly dressed. The Maine Hunting Shoe is designed by a hunter who has tramped the Maine woods for the past 18 years. We guarantee them to give perfect satisfaction in every way."

The public could not resist the common sense logic and genuine enthusiasm of his appeal. Success was starting to come. L. L. had learned the value of personally testing his products, of honest adver-

Leon A. Gorman.

tising based on firm convictions, and of keeping the customer satisfied at all cost.

By 1924 he was employing 25 people at an average wage of $25 a week. His sales totaled $135,000. By 1927 he had added fishing and camping equipment to his catalog. "It is no longer necessary for you to experiment with dozens of flies to determine the few that will catch fish," he wrote. "We have done that experimenting for you."

Word of mouth advertising and customer satisfaction were critical to L. L.'s way of thinking. "We consider our customers a part of our organization," he stated in his catalog, "and want them to feel free to make any criticism they see fit in regard to our merchandise or service." To hear that one of his products failed was a genuine shock to his system. He'd charge around the factory trying to find an explanation. Then he'd write the customer, return his money, enclose a gift, invite him fishing or do anything to make the matter right. That customer was a real person to L. L. and he'd put his trust in L. L.'s catalog.

By 1950, sales were $1,848,000, and in 1951 L. L. opened his retail store 24 hours a day, 365 days a year. "We have thrown away the keys to the place," he boomed. In 1954, he opened a ladies' department, and in 1956, he acquired the Small-Abbott moccasin factory. L. L. was in his eighties during this period and starting to slow down. His company was growing older with him and sales leveled off around the $2 million mark throughout the late fifties and early sixties.

L. L. died in 1967 at the age of 94. Business and pleasure had been one and the same for him. In his own words, L. L.'s business philosophy was: "Sell good merchandise at a reasonable profit, treat your customers like human beings, and they'll always come back for more." L. L. had enjoyed every minute of it.

I showed up for a job in 1961. I'd had a fine liberal arts education at Bowdoin College followed by four exciting years as an officer on Navy destroyers. More to the point, I was L. L.'s grandson and he'd always had a soft spot for unemployed relatives. He put me on the payroll at $80 per week.

In a way it was fortunate I had no prior experience. The only business principles I could learn were those L. L. had practiced for 50 years. His deep rooted beliefs in practical, tested products for outdoors people and in giving complete customer satisfaction were accepted by me as the only way to run a business. His catalog production methods, his style of writing copy, his advertising techniques for getting new customers and his conservative financing became the basis of my business education.

L. L. had staked out the basic product groups we continue today: outdoors apparel and footwear for men and women; hunting, fishing, camping, canoeing, and winter sports equipment; and casual apparel, footwear, and camp furnishings that L. L. and his customers liked and used. His "core product" was and is today, the "Maine Hunting Shoe." Everything else was consistent in quality and value with it.

Like many great entrepreneurs, however, L. L. had never been able to delegate any responsibilities or plan for any future beyond his own. During the fifties and early sixties his company was suffering from a lack of management and direction. His product groups were right, but the specific products were getting out of date and there were lapses in quality. Service was becoming erratic and the catalogs and advertising were repetitive and losing their effectiveness.

I studied the old catalogs, talked with the long-time employees and vendors, got seriously involved in hunting, fishing and our other outdoor product areas, and took many evening business courses at the University of Maine in Portland. I also absorbed as much as I could from L. L. himself. The process was one of total immersion in learning about our products and our markets.

L. L.'s original space advertising formula was sound and we made it work again with better data analysis, media selection, and the use of coupons.

Most importantly, we completely overhauled our personnel policies.

L. L.'s thinking placed the payroll about halfway between a reward system for work performed and a charitable contribution. We increased it to levels that were more than competitive in our area and included an equitable job rating system and a companywide performance bonus. We started attracting and retaining better people. In 1961 the average age of our employees was over 60. In 1975 it was in the forties. We added pension, savings and group life insurance programs. We implemented professional training courses for our supervisors. Communications and working conditions were substantially improved. The momentum of our growth provided ever increasing opportunities for individual advancement.

We had high morale and high motivation, fully committed to L. L.'s principles. Most of us enjoyed the outdoors and we'd started regular product testing trips to the Allagash and other parts of Maine's back country. We liked what we were doing in our business, believed it was very worthwhile to society, and did our best to build on it in every way. We had no long term debt and our management style was still very much in the entrepreneurial manner.

Our most important marketing efforts were in the areas of list acquisition and list activation. In 1976 we made extensive market surveys among our customers to determine their age, education and income demographics to assist us in our media selection. We also wanted to learn how our customers really felt about L. L. Bean so we wouldn't change anything they liked but could improve any areas where we were weak.

In acquiring new buyers, we carefully analyzed our costs in order to determine how much we could afford to invest in new names. We developed return on promotion and lifetime value techniques. We also developed extremely accurate methods for measuring results. Four hundred thousand outside names were tested in late 1975. The program was successful and by 1980 we were renting nearly five million outside names. This acquisition program added significantly to our buyer list which numbered 2.2 million in 1980 and it was a key factor in our growth since 1975.

We had recognized early on, however, that customer service and favorable word-of-mouth advertising were still the critical elements in any success we were to achieve with our activation and acquisition programs. This meant a lot of attention to timely order fulfillment, to personal responses to customer requests and problems, and to consistently high levels of product quality. We had observed too many others in the mail order industry who had failed to achieve satisfactory growth because of an over-concentration on sales and merchandising. They neglected the less glamorous, but essential, operational areas of the business which meant satisfaction to the customer and, ultimately, success.

We were increasingly involved in meeting our social responsibilities. We made substantial contributions to worthy health, welfare, arts, and civic projects. We put particular emphasis on environmental efforts in Maine and played a significant role in preserving the St. John River. Many of our people were actively involved in these community and environmental organizations.

Our story had been written up in such major publications as *Reader's Digest*, *The New York Times*, and *People* magazine. We'd appeared on the nationally televised "Today" show and on "Who's Who" with Dan Rather. We were highly conscious of the L. L. Bean image and had done our best to preserve L. L.'s principles and to maintain our continuity with the past.

Of these efforts, Ms. McNear said in her previously quoted article: "Some part of the success story that's built this place has to do with being in the right place at the right time . . . but a large part of the story is, after all these years—after computers and automation and seven million dollars poured into expansion, after the wisest marketing and production techniques—still about old-fashioned words like 'reliability' and 'responsibility' and *Bean's revolutionary idea of caring enough to treat a customer as a human being.*"

By Leon A. Gorman.
From the article,
L. L. Bean, Inc.: Outdoor
Specialties by Mail
from Maine (Princeton:
The Newcomen Society
in North America, 1981)

Justin Williams remembers the concern among Bean's customers when
L. L. died. They asked the same questions and shared the same doubts as
many of the employees.

Justin: A lot of these customers knew I'd been with Bean's for years and
years, you know, and they'd come up to me for my opinion about the company's future. And this went on well into the seventies. L. L. was a legend in
his own time, and it took a while before people could believe that things
around here wouldn't change. So, I'd tell them that L. L.'s grandson was
running the place now, and if they had put it on a computer they couldn't
have picked a better man. Usually, it was the older customers who wanted
to know about Leon. I think they felt insecure. And sometimes I'd chat with
them for four or five minutes, you know, and take care of other customers
at the same time, and the first thing you'd know there'd be a gang there, just
listening.

Me: I know. It's happened to me a few times.

Justin: And they'd thank me. I'd tell them that as long as Leon Gorman
is alive, this place will be run as L. L. would run it. Because the decisions
Leon makes are so near what I know L. L. would have done that it's literally
scary. Now, L. L. would climb over rocks and go right to the wall for his
people. Leon is the same way. And I'd tell the customers another thing—
that the 100% guarantee is going to stay. It's as solid as the Rock of Gibralter.
There's no way that's going to change. If L. L. were alive today, and up on
his computers and so forth, he could be Leon's double. Each Leon would be
a double of the other.

Me: I think you're right, from what I've seen.

Justin: There is no doubt in my mind at all on that.

Me: How wonderful it is, too.

Me: It is . . . and when customers hear that, they light right up! Of
course, I was the first sounding board. They knew I was there and would
kick out information.

Anna Williams notes some of the few—but major—differences between L. L. and Leon Gorman:

Anna: I didn't work around L. L. too much, but enough, you'd think, to be recognized. He was a funny guy . . . just as nice and dear as he could be, but he had his quirks. Idalyn worked with L. L. every day, and one morning she went into his office and said, "Hello, Mr. Bean," and he thought she was a customer. I'm sure he didn't know me from a hole in the ground. Leon seems to remember everybody.

Me: Did L. L. ever talk to you about your work?

Anna: No. But Leon did.

Me: What's he like to work for?

Anna: Leon was wonderful! But more exacting than L. L. Leon pulled you up. I used to write some of the advertising for the newspaper and the Ladies Department, and he sure straightened me out on that. I was of the generation that used a lot of adjectives, and he wanted it briefer and more concise. But, the nice way he went about correcting me, I thought the world of him. And when he was coming into the presidency, there was so much discussion among the help. Oh, yes. They were all fussing about this or that.

Me: Because he was a relative?

Anna: Partly. But mostly because they thought Leon didn't know anything about the business . . . a young fellow like him. I told them the way I felt about it, that we were lucky to have him. They could have sold the company and we'd all be wiped out. Well, they found out Leon was pretty quick to catch on. And a nice guy. And he was good to my son, Jerry. Jerry had applied for a summer job in the Sales Room and the Sales Room manager promised it to him. And then I guess the manager forgot about it, because when Jerry went in to report for work, the manager told him they were all filled up. Well, it was a good thing Jerry wasn't a bit like his mother . . . he had his father's spunk . . . and he waltzed himself right up to Leon's office and told him what had happened. And Leon saw to it that Jerry got a job. It wasn't in the Sales Room, but he got his summer job at Bean's. I never forgot that. I always liked Leon, and I was thankful he took the company and improved it, and I appreciate how he treats the employees.

Me: Are there any funny anecdotes about Leon?

Anna: Not that I know of. But there's a funny story about Tom Gorman, Leon's brother. He's an awfully nice guy, too. It runs in the family. And he's quiet, like Leon. That quietness is another way L. L. and Leon are different. L. L. was a real bull. Anyway, Tom used to race cars and travel around the country and he'd often take Jerry with him. This all leads up to the fact that he'd come back from these trips and bring movies with him. I didn't have a movie screen, but I'd put up this sheet in the living room and we'd have a regular show. Well, by gosh, I lost the sheet. And this day he'd just come back with more movies and he wanted to show them. So, I had to turn him down, but I hunted for the sheet and finally found it. So, Mary and myself and Idalyn were sitting there during the noon hour, and I happened to look down the street and there was Tom ambling along. I threw up the window and hollered, "Tommy!" And he looked around. And I hollered again, and he looked up, and I yelled out, "I found the sheet and you can come up tonight!" Well, he dusted into a store like sixty. The girls about died. I said, "Well, he's just gonna show movies."

So—the transition from L. L. to Leon was made. The employees (the downstairs) shrugged off their nervousness within a few months, their jobs secure, the company intact and little change noticeable. There was a general sadness around the place; the booming voice of L. L. had been replaced by the far gentler (but just as firm) monotones of Leon, and the idiosyncrasies of L. L., which gave rise to so many humorous incidences and anecdotes, were supplanted by a smoother, more predictable routine—and we learned, in time, that it was also an infinitely more efficient routine.

Leon Gorman had his work cut out for him. Replacing a genuine, greatly loved patriarch and one-of-a-kind character was no easy task, and, as he

Leon Gorman (left) and
L. L. Bean.
PORTRAIT BY EUGENE FULLER

points out in his Newcomen article, he was very much aware of it and even doubted at one point that he could do it.

But, as his brand of leadership took hold, and sales grew, and job security seemed more valid than ever, the downstairs couldn't help but notice and take heart. More important than the business results, however, was the character of the man, and it was here that, day by day, in his quiet way, Leon won the liking and trust of the employees. That was his toughest job, and he accomplished it in far shorter time than anyone would have thought. Every human and decent quality L. L. had put into his company was evident in Leon Gorman, and it was this, more than all the rising sales curves, that earned him the trust of the employees.

In one of my interviews with Leon concerning material for this book, I mentioned the appreciation the employees had for Leon's carrying on the L. L. tradition. And he said, "Well, you people have done as much as I have."

If any reader has any worry about the retention of this company's traditional character under Leon Gorman's leadership, forget it.

8

The More Things Change

One morning last spring, I spotted a long-ago customer among the crowds in the retail store. I hadn't seen this woman for nearly thirty years, but she had frequently shopped at Bean's during the fifties and sixties and I had waited on her many times. It took me a few moments to verify her identity in my mind and connect her with that bygone era, but there was no mistake; this was the charming and still very beautiful Miss S. W. who had turned the head of many a Beansman as she browsed her way through the store three decades ago.

I walked up to her and introduced myself, and she remembered me immediately. We reminisced for a few minutes and then she asked me to walk along with her a while as she looked over the counters. She told me she'd married and moved to Wyoming in the sixties. "I've ordered from the catalog since then," she said, "but this is the first time I've been in the store in all these many, many years."

"It's certainly changed a lot," I said.

"Well, it's bigger," she answered, "and more impressive, and there's an almost endless selection to choose from. All of that is different than it used to be. But, you know, the atmosphere and the feeling are the same. I was here for maybe a half-hour before you came by, and everybody's just as full of help and pleasantness as they used to be. That part of it hasn't changed a bit. It's still the same friendly Bean's to me. I half expect Mr. Bean to come bouncing down the stairs."

Hearing that from someone who hadn't been in the store for nearly thirty years is impressive. She was a customer when the Bean reputation for outstanding customer service was in full flower. "Hasn't changed a bit," she said.

Amen.

Remember my telling you about Ed Dwyer who delivered the camp stove to the lady in Vermont before she made her trip to Ireland? Well, that sort of thing still happens. Maxine Herling, one of our recent customer service representatives, took an excited call from a man in New Hampshire who had received a tent from us that was missing one pole. He was ready to leave on vacation and there was no time to mail one to him.

"Well, we had to make this customer happy," said Maxine, "so Ruthie Turner and I drove to Kittery with the pole."

Sounds like the old days, doesn't it?

Then there's the recent story of the man who was hanging around the store, not buying anything, just sort of walking up and down the aisles, and he kept on this way for so long that someone finally came up to him and asked what was going on (nicely, of course).

The reason he gave was that his wife had just left him, and when he'd stopped at the retail store on his way back to his home in Canada he was treated so nicely he just wanted to stick around a while. "I felt human for the first time in a month," he said, "and I didn't want to leave."

That has got to be one of the greatest testimonials to customer relations I've ever heard.

The days are long gone when L. L. used to stumble on the outside stairs on his way up to the office. He invariably did this, and it was our notification that "Grandpa" had arrived and that we'd better look busy. This quaint awareness of everything going on in the company—the mark of a small business in close quarters—died out many years ago, but the "family" mindset that developed in those days is alive and well and as strong as ever. You can sense it in the atmosphere around Bean's. It's entirely different from most businesses. The large majority of employees I run into—even the shortest-term, part-time workers—are quick to adopt good feelings toward Bean's, and they just as quickly and instinctively develop a protective concern for the company's image that goes well beyond the basic attitude expected of them in their jobs. A few of us got into that subject at lunch the other day, and a number of related anecdotes popped up:

The L. L. Bean building in 1935. Note the outside stairs. L. L. would invariably stumble on these stairs when he came to work in the morning— our signal to look busy.

. . . A young woman we'd just hired was walking through the parking lot on her way to lunch one day and saw a big package fall off the roof rack of a bright red Chevy station wagon that was leaving the lot. She shouted at the driver, who apparently didn't hear her, so she picked up the package and examined the outside of it for some sort of identification. There was nothing on it at all, so she put it in her car and then spent her entire lunch hour driving around Freeport in hopes of finding the station wagon. She finally spotted it at a restaurant and had the manager page the owner of the car. He came out, got the package and offered her a twenty-dollar bill with what she described as "five minutes of thanks." (She did not accept the money.) There's no doubt that this employee probably would have searched for the owner of the package anyway, but when she was asked about it later, she said: "Well, I couldn't have this man thinking his package was stolen in Bean's parking lot!"

. . . A customer called up one day, practically in tears. She had lost her "little green frog." She had put it in the box that had come with a pair of shoes she'd ordered from us. She had then returned the shoes to us for some reason or other, but she had forgotten to retrieve the frog from the box. Our operator called the Receiving Department, and everybody started looking for this frog. When the operator returned from lunch a day or so later, there, on her desk, was a little green *ceramic* frog. She rushed the frog out to Shipping, saw to it that it was packed with extreme care, checked on the shipping date and then telephoned the customer in a few days to be sure the frog had arrived safely. The customer was ecstatic! She had been sure—positive—that she'd seen the last of her little green frog. (If she had mailed it to any other large company, she probably would have been right. Can you imagine the operator at a big company taking a personal interest in finding a lost *frog?* And not only was the Bean operator determined to find that frog, but Receiving and Shipping were equally determined to find and return it.)

. . . One of our summer workers, a college student, was fishing in New Jersey in early fall and happened to be standing near a young boy whose rod broke. The boy was heartbroken and said he'd just received the rod from L. L. Bean and didn't have money for another one. Our college student assured the youngster that Bean's would replace the rod immediately, but he sensed the boy didn't believe him, so he accompanied the boy to his nearby home and received permission from the boy's mother to make a long-distance call to Freeport. He told Bean's what had happened, related the assurances he'd given the boy, then waited while Bean's confirmed the original order and verified that a replacement rod would be shipped that same day. I don't need to tell you how happy that boy must have been— and all of this, I want to remind you, was carried out by a student who had worked for us for only two months during the previous summer.

To my mind, the funniest story about how Bean employees go out of their way for customers was told to me by a man I met recently at a business conference. It seems his daughter, Jenny, and some of her friends had driven to Bean's one night to do some back-to-college shopping. It was quite late when they finished, and they discovered they'd locked their keys in the car. While they were deciding what to do, a Bean employee, a young man, over-heard the problem as he was leaving the building and offered to help. "He seemed a little hesitant," said Jenny. "He said something like . . . 'Uh . . . er . . . I could . . . uh, help you, I guess, but you mustn't say anything, you know.'" Jenny didn't have any idea what the hesitancy was about, but any help was fine with her. Anyway, the Bean employee went to his own car and came back in a few moments with a *professional* unlocking tool like the police use (a long, flat, very thin metal rod with a special lock-opening notch at the bottom). He inserted it between the window and the outer door panel and had the door open in an instant. Jenny thanked him for his trouble, but all our hero wanted was for her to forget about the incident.

When I told this story, one of the women at the table said, "Oh, I know that kid. He works for one of those car-towing outfits on weekends. He must have had his tool kit with him that night. I guess he's not allowed to use that door-opener unless it's official business."

I'll have to tell Jenny's dad about that; I'm sure Jenny would like to know how a Bean employee stuck his neck out to give her a helping hand.

The old saying "The more things change, the more they stay the same" has been very true in respect to the people who work for Bean's, and I include both employees and management. Many outward things about the company have changed as a result of growth and technology, but the nature of Bean's personnel, from top to bottom, has remained as constant and reliable as the quality of the Maine Hunting Shoe. In this respect, a customer of the forties or fifties, as mentioned a few pages back, would feel right at home at today's L. L. Bean, Inc. One solid reason for this is management's intuitive empathy with the traditions established by L. L. In their hearts—and that's where it counts—Bean's management agrees with the standards set by L. L. It isn't something they have to learn; they just have it inside them. It is this that has kept the Bean tradition alive and well, and it is this that is responsible for the caliber of personnel we attract, the quality of our goods and the maintenance of a reputation among customers that is arguably the best of any company in America. From top to bottom, this company really *cares*, and it is a rare job applicant going on our payroll who hasn't demonstrated that spirit to the instinctive satisfaction of the person responsible for the hiring.

In L. L.'s day, employee attitude training was at first nonexistent, but was then implemented gradually as the company grew larger and L. L. couldn't personally "size up" every applicant. Today, of course, with thousands of employees, such training is standard. Given the informal character analysis in the initial interview, however, employee training is largely a matter of reinforcing the applicant's good qualities and instilling knowledge of the company's history and methods of doing business. In short, when a job

applicant appears to be the kind of person we want working for us—
someone with a heart and mind in the proper place—the employee training
serves to put such assets to work for the company. As I said in the first
chapter of this book, no amount of training can teach someone to be
thoughtful, caring and concerned. If those qualities aren't already built into
a job applicant's psyche, the chances are excellent we'll spot it in the initial
interview and that person won't be working for Bean's. And that tradition
has been kept alive by a management that has exactly the same qualities it is
looking for in its applicants: thoughtfulness, caring and concern.

    Just as basic hiring practices have remained the same, assuring customers

*Shoe Department in our
factory salesroom, 1956.
That's me, acting like a
customer, at lower right.*

of the uniquely personable services they've always received from Bean's, so, too, have most of the company's fundamental philosophies. Leon Gorman, for example, doesn't have to go into the woods to try out Bean's products the way L. L. did—but he does—and he takes company executives along with him. Why does he do it? Because it's still the best way to test our products and assure our customers that they work as advertised. Nobody ever invented a surer way to offer a product honestly. Another purpose is to keep Bean's executives appreciative of the great outdoors and to personally familiarize them with the uses of Bean's outdoor products. In today's world, there is precious little time for top-level management to leave desks and duties and computers and head off on work-week excursions through woods and fields and down rivers and up mountains. At Bean's, it's part of the job. And it is by no means always a picnic. Canoeing the Allagash Wilderness Waterway, for instance, may develop camaraderie and reacquaint executives with one another, but it can also be miserably cold, wet and occasionally dangerous. It is, however, extraordinarily instructive—and that's why it's done.

In all the ways that count, then, L. L. Bean, Inc. is very much the same as it was in L. L.'s era, and "the ways that count" have to do with people and attitudes and personal and business philosophies. The company may be a dozen times larger and the epitome of a high-tech operation in a modern world, but its dealings with customers remain as neighborly and straight-forward as they were in the days when L. L. would walk around the place straightening up the shelves and giving advice to a boy who was buying his first pocketknife. Every customer—whether buying in person or by mail, whether buying a little or a lot—senses in his or her bones that they are not only valued, but *liked*. And that is a distinct rarity in this day and age. It is also no change from the way L. L. Bean, Inc. has done business since 1912.

John Hughes, the Pulitzer Prize-winning journalist, commented on all of this in an article he wrote for the *Christian Science Monitor* on August 8, 1985:

In a world swirling with change, we have just received for our annual summer reading that reassuring symbol of security and continuity, the L. L. Bean fall catalog.

It is doubly welcome this year, for our household has recently had a couple of bad jolts: A number of our favorite trading houses are going out of business or changing hands, and a couple of mail-order catalogs we've known over the years will no longer be issued. Even more disorienting has been the monstrosity just perpetrated by the New England Telephone Company on the cover of our new phone directory. For years, the Cape Cod edition has been published with a rustic New England photo on the cover. This year the phone book has been re-done; the rustic picture has been replaced by a surrealistic design of mangled reds, greens, and oranges.

There has been a fine pother about all this. Quite a few local columns have appeared, none of them complimentary. There has been a slew of letters to the newspapers crackling with that outraged ire of which New Englanders are capable when longtime institutions are under attack.

And so it has been reassuring to get the familiar catalog in the mail from Freeport, Maine, and to learn that nothing is changing in the world of L. L. Bean.

It is full once again of the things that I will probably never buy, but which conjure up pictures of simple woodsmen, warm wool plaid against their chests, out with their dogs in the forest, beyond reach of recorded telephone messages, computer printouts, and music they don't like with lyrics they can't stand.

Indeed, the cover shows just such a woodsman in the background, his dog dominating the autumnal foreground. The dog is a Brittany spaniel, said by L. L. Bean to be "pointing for woodcock." You can't see the woodcock, and the dog may be faking it, hoping to get this nonsense over quickly and get back to the warm fire. But the camaraderie between man and dog gives the reader a satisfying feeling.

Inspecting fabric quality in our in-house laboratory. (Courtesy Bernard Carpenter)

All the well-known items are in the catalog—pages and pages of boots, and dozens and dozens of parkas and Maine flannel shirts and corduroy trousers. The instructions for ordering remain common-sensical: For footwear, "enclose outline of bare foot. Hold pencil straight up when tracing foot." Also, "advise type of stockings (light, heavy, etc.) you plan to wear." For hats and caps, measure in inches "around the largest part of the head with tape above brow ridges." It's important to get that tape above those brow ridges.

There is an improved parka fabric that has been tested for more than double the abrasion resistance of lesser parkas. It was tested on a special abrasion-creating machine at 1,000 revolutions, and there is a color picture of the technician actually being abrasive.

Lots of L. L. Bean's clothing and sleeping bags are filled with prime-quality goose down. To the casual observer, goose down is goose down. But L. L. Bean's down is "tested continuously," hand-separated in an eight-hour process, then weighed and checked under magnification to ensure that it is high-quality down from high-quality geese.

The next step is testing for "fill power," which measures the ability of the down to "loft and trap air." L. L. Bean has serious standards. A one-ounce sample of goose down must "loft to at least 550 cu. in." Presumably down that doesn't loft right is tossed out, and the family of geese from which it came is on L. L. Bean's black list.

The company also has a black sheep, the black Welsh mountain sheep, whose wool is used, unbleached and undyed, to make sweaters. The black Welsh mountain sheep, L. L. Bean informs us chattily, is the only all-black sheep in Britain and has been used there for wool "since the Middle Ages."

L. L. Bean hasn't been around that long, of course, but in a world where change is inevitable, its quaint durability is soothing.

One of the wonderful things that has never changed around Bean's is the sense of humor of the employees, but that's to be expected, because humor is generally a built-in attribute of people who like other people. The one story that never fails to break up the ladies at Bean's has been going around for nearly twenty years now, and it happened to Maxine Herling, who was the source of an anecdote reported earlier in this chapter. Funny things had a habit of happening to this bouyant lady:

Maxine: An older gentleman called me one day about his trousers. He said he had a complaint. I asked him what it was. I could tell he was maybe eighty or so.

Older Gentleman: Well, it's about the opening. You know, the fly. It's not long enough.

Maxine: Excuse me?

Older Gentleman: The fly's not long enough. I need a longer opening. Much longer!

Maxine (on the verge of laughter, trying to control herself): Er . . . uh . . . all right. How much longer?

Older Gentleman: Oh, I don't know, five or six inches, I guess, whatever you can . . .

At which point Maxine couldn't handle it any more and had to turn away from the phone roaring with laughter.

Mention it to her today and she busts up. Totally.

9

"Here Come the Beans"

A mong some Maine forest rangers, the yearly throng of backpackers, hikers, canoeists and other folk fleeing to the wilderness for a few days of respite are known—not unkindly—as "Beans."

By the seventies, the national interest in fitness and healthy outdoor activities had led to specialized buying patterns that represented a large part of Bean's business. This was in addition, of course, to the traditional market composed of hunters, fishermen, farmers and others whose outdoor occupations demanded the sturdy, functional clothing and products offered by the company. Although the need for product dependability was the same for both markets, the new trends required different orientations. Bicycles and kayaks, for instance, for vacationers, or camping equipment designed for family outings rather than for lone trappers who might spend several months in the deep northern woods. To call the new breed of customer a "leisure" user might fit the description in some other companies, and products for such users might be downgraded accordingly—but not at

Bean's. Product integrity was to remain paramount regardless of how the product was to be used, whether it was cross-country skis for a business person on a weekend outing or a raincoat for a full-time Maine guide. Customers quickly recognized this adherence to product integrity, and in time it became more likely than not that when vacationers took to the woods, trails and lakes, they would be equipped in some measure with L. L. Bean goods. As the forest rangers said, such people were "Beans." (But, of course, so were the rangers.)

There were times, of course, when the product lines would overlap and when there was little difference between leisure use and professional use.

One "leisure" customer complained that he'd been snowshoeing in northern Canada during a New Year's week vacation and had met up with a professional hunter who wore the same snowshoes he'd been sold. His complaint was that he had obviously been sold snowshoes designed for heavy-duty wear, not a brief vacation.

His complaint was quite true. He had come into the store for his purchase, and when he explained to one of our customer representatives that he planned to fly to a rented cabin on a frozen lake fifty or so miles from the nearest settlement and then trek around the surrounding area on his snowshoes, communing with nature, our rep made sure he had the toughest and most proven pair of snowshoes in the place—the same kind we'd sold to hunters and trappers in that remote, unforgiving region. If he'd been planning to dance around in his backyard, that would have been another matter. All we were trying to do was keep this customer alive. We told him that, and he settled down. We would have been perfectly willing, of course, to give him his money back.

A couple of years ago, a retired couple bought some light camping equipment from us for an occasional "warm weather weekend" in their nearby state forest in Virginia. That's what they told us. As it turned out, they de-

cided to take their first vacation in Vermont, on a weekend in late October, and were caught in a minor blizzard that kept them confined to their tent for three days in below-freezing temperatures.

"Real good gear," wrote the man. "Everything worked like a charm. The Warden looked in on us a couple of times a day, and when he saw the L. L. Bean label on our stuff he told us not to worry about it not working right."

The equipment we sold to that couple would have been classified as "leisure," but always and without fail this company does its best to provide products with built-in performance that goes a bit beyond the expected.

I remember one time, though, when one of our products didn't live up to the user's expectations.

A young man had come in with a hunting knife he'd bought from us. The handle was all scratched up and about a half-inch of the tip was missing. I was the first one he ran into, so he explained what had happened:

Young Man: This knife is really out of balance.

Me: Out of balance?

Young Man: Yeah, I can't hit a thing with it.

Me: You throw it at things?

Young Man: You know, like those Malayan daggers . . . throwing knives . . . the kind the marines use.

Me: Well, I think those are special knives. I mean, they're designed for throwing. That's what they're made for.

Young Man: Nobody told me I *couldn't* throw it! It's not balanced right. I wouldn't have bought it if I'd known that.

Me: It looks like you've been throwing it at rocks.

Young Man: Not on purpose! It kept missing the tree all the time and going off to one side or the other. Boy, I'll tell you, it's terrible to try and throw this thing. Makes me look like a jerk.

I didn't say so, but I had to agree with him on that last part. I saw to it he got his money back.

To accommodate the truly meteoric rise of the company's business in the past twenty years, due in large measure to the "discovery" of L. L. Bean by Americans of all ages and life-styles heading for fun and fitness in the Great Outdoors, our jobs at the company became more and more high-tech. Terms such as data-processing and facsimile transmission became standard job profiles, and questions about computer familiarity and expertise became as normal on job application requirements as typing speed was in the old days.

But, like the local employees who came off the farms in the early days and quickly learned to adapt to the then-modern demands of a going business, we've managed to do the same today. This is not to say we haven't had our share of glitches in the operation of high-tech equipment. . . .

Consider the case of C. W., who took an order for ten pairs of socks. Another employee happened to glance at her screen at the very moment she was entering the order, and said, "Boy! Now that's a *real* order!"

"Oh, I don't know," said C. W. I had one for a couple of dozen this morning."

"No, I mean the one for ten thousand."

The way things were in pre-computer days.

*Our main computer room
in 1982. (Courtesy Deb
McLean)*

"What ten thousand?" asked C.W., rereading her screen. "Oh my goodness! I must have held the key down. Thank you! Thank you!"

That's the kind of mistake you couldn't have made with most typewriters.

When a bunch of us were talking about this sort of thing one day, somebody mentioned that she'd once received an electric bill for over seven million dollars. "I laughed," she said, "and sent it back with a note telling the company I couldn't understand such a high bill, because I'd told my kids not to leave the night-light on."

The serious switchover to computer technology took place in the seventies and, of course, continues to this day. We have our own training programs, and I'm happy to say that our employee turnover rate in Data Processing is about a tenth of that for the industry as a whole.

I remember a typist being introduced for the very first time to a computer. She was a loyal Bean employee, extremely good at her job, but had no use or love for anything but her trusty typewriter. This is about how I remember her reaction:

L. D.: Look, I learned how to use a typewriter when the only thing I knew was how to milk cows. I learned how to sort out a mailing list and keep everything in order when the only office experience I'd ever had was at a table in the kitchen making out milk, cream and butter bills. It was a big deal when we added eggs; I had to redesign the whole system. I may not be the smartest person in the world, but I can tell you I can do everything on this typewriter you can do on that computer and do it better and faster. I've learned all I need to learn, and at my age I don't figure to spend the rest of my days staring at a television screen. If my typewriter breaks, I can fix it. If this thing breaks, I'd never know what to do. If I make a mistake on my typewriter, it's between me and the typewriter. I hear that if you make a mistake on this thing, everybody knows about it. And if you make a real bad mistake, you get a zillion labels with the wrong information. If you want mailing lists that are accurate and neat and on-time, you want me at my type-writer. I don't know what you'll get out of this contraption.

And, with that, she stomped off to her typewriter.

I thought she did a good job of stating her opinion, and I can assure you it was shared by a lot of us.

But—also like a lot of us—the countless benefits of the computer became obvious as time passed. We worked for a company that allowed us to make high-tech transitions at our own pace, and I believe they understood that we had the company's benefit in mind. We thought we could do our jobs better with the old, familiar equipment, and they respected that and gave us time to learn and accommodate ourselves to the new systems. Nobody said, "Learn this or you're fired!" In effect, what they said was, "Well, take a look at it and learn how it works."

That's what we did, and except for very few holdouts, there was no denying that we could serve the rapidly growing company far more efficiently with modern equipment. L. D. left the company several years ago, and the last time I saw her she was humming a tune to herself as she was wiping the dust off her monitor.

The increasing use of Bean's products for fitness, health and leisure has led to some amusing situations:

One of our older employees, a man who spent much of his life helping hunters and fishermen select proper gear, stepped up to help a man whom he described as ". . . built like a bear, hadn't shaved for a few days and looked like he lived on Mt. Katahdin."

"Looking for some pants," said the customer.

"Right this way," said our rep, leading the customer to an area filled with the hardiest backwoods clothing known to man. "Tell me just what you need and I'll show you what we have."

"Something I can use for a tournament," said the man.

"Tournament? Oh, you mean log-rolling or something."

"No," said the customer. "A croquet tournament."

"Excuse me."

"Croquet. You know, the game. Nothing here looks suitable . . . too woodsy, you know. Not at all fitting."

Our rep was stunned. If ever there was a customer who appeared to have just stepped out of the backwoods, this was the one. He said later it was the biggest misjudgment he had ever made. The customer was a Yale professor in search of a pair of light slacks, preferably in green, with socks to match.

Then there was the man who called up and wanted information on the warmest parka we had. "Going into some real cold weather," he told our customer representative. "Need the best thing you've got."

Our rep recommended our top-of-the-line parkas, the kind often purchased by Maine guides and other professionals for extended use in temperatures ranging to forty below zero.

"Think that'll do it?" asked the customer. "I mean, it gets *cold* where I'm going!"

"And just where are you going?" asked our rep.

"Over to Arkansas," said the customer. "Going horseback riding in the hills and I hear it gets below freezing sometimes."

Needless to say, our rep switched his recommendations.

It's wonderful to watch the variety of people who shop at Bean's these days. There's nothing predictable about it. Thirty or forty years ago, our clientele was largely composed of people who worked outdoors or who hunted, fished or trapped. Today it's entirely different, and I always look forward to what a new workday may bring in the way of customers.

A middle-aged man, bent over from severe arthritis, came in looking for a pair of skis recently. The person who waited on him couldn't have imagined what this man wanted with skis, but he explained that he wanted to learn the sport. "Just for easy cross-country," he said. "I'm already molded into the bent-forward position, so I ought to be pretty good."

Bean Touring Bicycle

Bean's Sport/Fitness Bicycle

64   Bean's Country Road Bicycle

L. L. Bean Bicycles

Considered by many experts to represent the leading edge in current bicycle design, function and value. Our product development team and one of America's premier bicycle manufacturers worked together to offer our customers this outstanding family of custom bicycles.

Each model is designed around the distinctive, large diameter, heat treated aluminum frame. Aluminum is stronger than even Reynolds 531 steel, lighter and much stiffer, allowing the most efficient transfer of energy from pedal to wheel. You will ride farther, faster and with less effort. The large diameter aluminum tubing also dampens shock better than steel for a smoother, more comfortable ride and precise cornering.

Our Bean Bicycles are made in the U.S.A. and outfitted with the highest quality components from Italy, England, France, Japan and the United States. Each frame is beautifully finished with DuPont® Imron® enamel paint process for a lifetime of protection. Each bicycle is fully tuned and packaged in a single large box. Assembly is simplified with enclosed instructions. Tools included. All L. L. Bean Bicycles are fully guaranteed.

Bean's Touring Bicycle

Designed and outfitted for touring around the country or around town. Full 15 speed gear range provides comfortable riding in any part of the country. Includes sturdy aluminum rear carrier, water bottle cage and one pint water bottle. Weight: 23" frame weighs 24 lbs. 6 oz.
Available in frame sizes: 19-21-23-25.

8246C Bean's Touring Bicycle, $595.00 plus $30.00 shipping and handling.

Bean's Sport/Fitness Bicycle

Our L. L. Bean aluminum alloy frame with the 12-speed Shimano 600EX Component Package, high-performance rims and tires for exceptional acceleration, cornering, straight-line speed and response. Designed for the person who bicycles for fitness or citizen racing. Wt.: 23" frame weighs 24 lbs.
Available in frame sizes: 19-21-23-25.

8241C Bean's Sport/Fitness Bicycle, $395.00 plus $30.00 shipping and handling.

Bean's Country Road Bicycle

Well suited for riding back country roads and logging or tote roads. Wide, shock absorbing tires and sturdy construction also withstand the punishment of city pot holes, storm grates and curbs. Frame is manufactured from the same heat treated aluminum alloy as our Touring and Sport Bicycles, in a thicker, all-terrain configuration. Extraordinarily strong and responsive for a bicycle so light in weight. Wide 10 gear range allows fast touring and excellent hill climbing.
Weight: 23" frame weighs 26 lbs. 6 oz.
Available in frame sizes: 16-18-21-23.

8295C Bean's Country Road Bicycle, $395.00 plus $30.00 shipping and handling.

Please send me your fully illustrated brochure on the complete family of L. L. Bean Aluminum Frame Bicycles.

Name_____
    First   Middle Initial   Last
Street_____Apt#_____
City_____State____Zip_____
Age_____

L. L. Bean catalog summer, 1985.

A young man on his way to college stopped by for a pair of "extra baggy" corduroy slacks. "It's the opposite of the 'in' look," he said, "but I'm betting the cost of these slacks that it will be 'in' before I leave school. You have to be prepared, you know."

A woman came in and spotted our Deer Carrier—a functional, no-nonsense cart for carrying dead deer out of the woods. "Can you paint it blue?" she asked. "I'd like to use it as a compost cart. All my other garden tools have blue handles."

Many times—many times—entire families come in and spend hours selecting equipment for camping vacations, everything from a tent to a compass. I stood by once while a family bought enough equipment to outfit a small logging camp. "I tried to keep it simple," said the person who waited on them, "but they wanted everything they saw. They're only going camping, but they wanted sleeping bags *and* blankets for everybody, and boots and moccasins, and two stoves, in case one broke, and just about everything else in the store. They bought three hatchets, three flashlights and—get this—*two* knife sharpeners. It's okay with me, but I sure tried to tell them they didn't need half the stuff they bought. I tell you the truth, I don't like sales like that. Makes me feel kind of guilty." (It makes *me* feel pretty good, though, to work with a man as caring as that—it's what Bean's is all about.)

I think what I like most about today's customers is the sheer joy they exude when they come into the store. Here, displayed around them, are all the marvelous things they've envisioned for whatever outdoor fun and exercise they have in mind. There is almost nothing they could need or want that Bean's doesn't carry. And look! Here it is! It's magical. Clothes, kayaks, skis, bicycles, fishing, hunting and camping gear, fitness and back-packing equipment . . . an endless list of wholesome, well-made products from a company that cares and wishes them well.

And, most of all, shares in their joy.

10

Precious Memories

At the time I'm writing this, I'm just five days away from my seventy-fifth birthday celebration. I plan to host a party with a gala get-to-gether of 750 invited guests—ten guests for every year of my life.

By the time you read this, my party will have been long over, but I want you to believe something. I want you to believe that I'm sorry I didn't know you. I would have invited you to the party. I mean that—indeed I do—and here's your invitation:

How to celebrate my 75th year of living?
Let's have a Birthday Fling!
It's a May Day Birthday Party
to celebrate our Birthdays.
I would love to have you join me
and our friends for
reminiscing and a general good time.
This is not a birthday party for me.
This is a party for us - to celebrate the
Spirit of Birth, Spring, life,
new and old friendships.

Bring Spring in with us:

JOIN: CARLENE GRIFFIN

WHEN: May 2, 1992

TIME: 8:00 p.m. til midnight

WHERE: Ballroom, Atrium Inn,
              Cooks Corner, Brunswick

RSVP by April 20th with the enclosed card.
PLEASE INCLUDE YOUR NAME AND GUEST.
Please, no presents only your presence!

For twenty years I've planned to write this book—to preserve (from the employees' viewpoint) the L. L. Bean Company that I knew and came to love. This love goes far beyond the necessities of working and making a living. I could have done that in many places. No, this book is about lives, and life spans, and the priceless good fortune that steered so many of us to spend it at a company such as this.

Now the manuscript is finished—and I don't know if I'm happy or sad. A little of both, I think. The desire to do this has been so strong, and so much a part of my life, that the completion of this book seems a little like retiring. And I am by no means ready for any such silly thing as retiring. Let's just call it precious memories.

As I drift back in time, I remember (how well I remember) taking the company's telegrams down to the Freeport train station in the mornings. That was more than fifty years ago, and it was an "honor" to be entrusted with the responsibility of going "down the hill" to the station. A little old man sat behind the counter, tapping out Morse code on the telegraph.

That train station played a big part in our company operations. Brown's truck would pick up packages from us and drive them down to the station, while one of us would follow the truck to pick up parcels that fell off. We had to do this every time, yelling at him to stop when a package tumbled to the street, and he'd get out of the truck and put the errant parcel on the front seat.

Freeport station—as a working depot—is long gone, but the building is still there, bought by some people in Boothbay who turned it into a museum. The FREEPORT sign is still hanging on it.

Today, of course, we have FAX machines that send documents everywhere in the world. And UPS and Federal Express for our packages. Fittingly, I'm the one who usually sends our FAXes—it's my current job at Bean's—but it's not as much fun as walking down the hill in the thirties to that little old man and listening to the tap-tap-tap-a-tap of incoming mes-

R. R. Station, Freeport, Me.

The Freeport Depot as the author remembers it from the thirties. (Courtesy Freeport Historical Society)

sages. At my age, life is supposed to be composed largely of nostalgia. I suppose it is, but it is happy nostalgia, I assure you. That train station is part of it.

Kippy Goldrup (whom I mentioned in the first chapter) was born in 1904 and has many memories and mementos of his days with Bean's. To talk with Kippy is to be transported back to the very first days of the L. L. Bean Com-

Kippy Goldrup and one of our Maine Hunting Shoes for an extra-large customer.

pany, even before my time. In my last interview with him in 1988, his recollections about L. L., his fellow employees, the operations of the company and the personalities of Freeport townspeople in the teens and twenties were as sharp and clear as if he were talking about current events. You can see it in some of the undirected talk we enjoyed during the interview:

Kippy: When I was in high school, Bean's used to get its boot rubbers from a manufacturer named Hood. The rubbers came in big wooden boxes, and we'd attach them just ahead of the heel on the Bean Hunting Shoe. L. L. made some modification to the process, but the point is that these boot rubbers came in big wooden boxes, and I know many of these boxes ended up as building materials for local homes.

Me: Yes, I've heard that.

Kippy: I've still got one of those boxes, and I'll show it to you later. For some reason, that reminds me of Nora Fitts. She can't still be alive, can she?

Me: Oh, yes. She's still alive (1988) and lives down near the overpass. The same old place. Bean's bought it and told her she could live there until she died. Bean's even bought her the stovewood she needed.

Kippy: That sounds like Bean's. I can remember when she used to bring lunches into Bean's for us to buy.

Me: She had the best crabmeat sandwiches you ever ate.

Kippy: I think crabmeat was forty cents a pound in the thirties.

Me: Do you remember John Gould, the writer?

Kippy: Sure. He was two years older than I was, so we weren't real chummy. I remember his mother was about the last person in town to accept sliced bread. "I guess I can slice my own bread," she used to say.

Me: Anything special you can tell me about L. L.?

Kippy: I could fill a book with L. L. stories, but what stands out most is that loud voice of his. He didn't need a telephone to call Portland; he just had to open the window!

Me: I bet you could actually hear him from as far away as Frank Merrill's livery stable.

Kippy: It was Harry who owned the stable. Frank worked for Bean's as a machinist.

Me: Oh, you're right . . .

And so it went . . . this old and gentle man, with as sharp a memory for details as anyone else I talked with in my many interviews for this book. Kippy was a link with the past, the very beginnings, and after the interview he took me out to a little cabin in the backyard and showed me the ancient Hood rubber box. Stenciled on the box was the misspelled word "Beane."

"It was always spelled that way," said Kippy. "The Hood boys never did get it right. We've used this box for storing preserves and that's why it's still around. It's a collector's item now, of course, and I hope my son will have room for it when I'm through using it. I don't want anything to happen to it."

Later that year, I took Kippy over to our Manufacturing Division for a visit. It had been many years since he'd been involved in the manufacturing process, and the moment we opened the door, and the smell of leather came to him, his eyes lit up and the adventure was on. It was a day I believe he'll never forget. "They don't use a cutting knife," he remarked at one point. "It's all done by clicker machines. 1400 pair a day. Good lord!"

For the most part, though, he was unusually quiet, turning things over in his mind, going back and forth between the way it had been and the way it was now. It was touching. And I felt it. He was the last of the originals, and if I could have turned the clock back to 1912, I would have done so. Gladly.

Kippy . . . George Soule . . . Dot Marston . . . Justin Williams and his big dog, Sandy . . . the names roll off easily, as familiar to me as the old Bean signs and buildings. L. L., himself, his huge voice echoing throughout the building, looms larger than life in my memories, and I know that I witnessed an era of entrepreneurship and old-line American standards and decencies that are preciously rare in the late twentieth century. As for the future, Justin

*Kippy Goldrup on his
nostalgic 1988 tour of our
Manufacturing Division.
That's me in black.*

Williams put it best when he compared Leon Gorman with L. L., as ". . . if they had put it on a computer." I had that quote in an earlier chapter, but it belongs in this last chapter as well, because it is in Leon Gorman, and those around him, that the legacy of this company will be continued and that the future can be fashioned to contain all the good and valuable things of the past. So far, so good. And it gives me the optimism and energy to live to 120 and take it all in, loving every minute of it.

Speaking of being 120, I conducted a hundred or more interviews in assembling material for this book, and, at one point, I set out to find one of the oldest people in Freeport for a real old-timer's view of the town. The man I located had never worked for Bean's, but he knew L. L., and I asked him for some nostalgic comments. He wasn't 120 years old, but I'll bet he was in his late nineties. This interview was in 1989, and for reasons that will become obvious, I won't use his name:

Old-Timer: Sure, I remember old L. L. . . . remember him when he first came to town. Yep. He'd stand in front of the store giving shoes away.

Me: He'd give shoes away?

Old-Timer: Oh, yeah. He'd ask you if you needed some shoes today, and then he'd give 'em to you. Got a pair myself. Real nice they were.

Me: I never heard that. I know he gave free shoes to the hobos during the Depression, but you mean he'd just give away shoes to everybody in town?

Old-Timer: Yep. L. L. made his reputation that way. Got all the Freeport folks to like him real well. I tell you, they didn't come any nicer than L. L.

Me: I've worked for Bean's for almost all my life and I never heard that story. Is there anyone else still around who saw him give away shoes to the townspeople?

Old-Timer: Oh, I don't know. Maybe. I was talking with L. L. about it just yesterday. Why don't you ask him? . . .

Needless to say, I ended the interview as quickly as possible. L. L. had been dead for twenty-two years. I suppose I should have told him, but whatever world the old-timer was living in I thought it best to leave him there.

Freeport, today, is a bustling little city—a far cry from the sleepy little village it was when L. L. first set up shop. In those days, when the fire bell would ring, most of our male employees would leave the customers standing in the aisles and go off to fight the fire. L. L. told them to do just that, and not to punch out on the time clocks. Nobody worried about theft, and the customers would generally understand and wait patiently for the salespeople to return.

Same with our all-night service. When it was first started, as an accommodation to hunters and fishermen who were traveling at night to get to the woods or blinds by early morning, we generally had just one or two men in the building. There was a sign on the door instructing customers to ring a bell. Sooner or later, the night man would open the door and, likely as not, offer the customer a cup of coffee while escorting him around the store. It was the epitome of casualness and neighborly business dealing, and it would probably be just the same today if it weren't for the sheer number of customers coming through the doors at all hours of the day and night.

Kippy Goldrup remembers when they first put up STOP signs on some of the side streets leading into Freeport's main thoroughfare. Well, that was an astounding thing in those days. *STOP* signs! In Freeport! And, sure enough, they put one up at the end of L. L.'s street. This was a grave insult to L. L. Here was an inanimate sign ordering him to regulate his driving. It was an invasion of his freedom, and there was no way he was going to subject himself to such an outlandish directive. "Well, I'm not going to stop my car once I get it started," said L. L. Cars had to be hand-cranked in those days, and they had a tendency to stall if they were stopped before they had a good chance to warm up. But that wasn't the main point; it was the prin-

Map from Bean's spring,
1952 catalog. L. L. was
concerned that the new
by-pass around Freeport
would affect his retail
trade, and he did his
best to point customers
in his direction.

ciple of the thing, and Kippy doesn't think L. L. ever did obey the STOP sign while he lived on that street, and that was for many years. Later, when the town's traffic had increased a hundredfold, I suppose he did obey STOP signs, but he would have done so reluctantly—even when it was obvious it was the only way to stay alive.

Freeport's traffic growth was largely brought on by the L. L. Bean Company, of course, and has its roots, in large measure, in L. L.'s determination to let people know where he was. This map is from the Spring catalog in 1952, and updated maps soon became a catalog tradition.

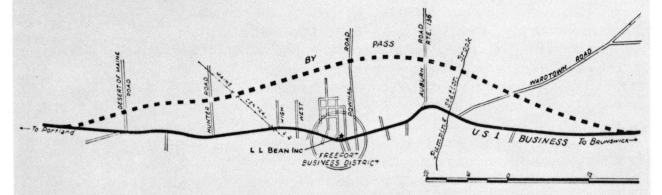

Freeport Three and One-Half Mile By-Pass

The new road around Freeport is longer and slower. There are three lights on the By-Pass and none on the straight U.S. 1 Business Highway through Freeport Village, as shown on the above map.

The By-Pass takes the truck traffic around Freeport, making the route through Freeport faster, safer and allows ample free parking. Even if you do not intend to stop, the route through our pleasant village will give you 5 minutes relaxation from heavy traffic strain.

Coming by toll road Freeport is the first shopping center east of Boston. Those who visited us last year will be surprised and pleased with the new atmosphere of quiet, easy shopping conditions.

Keep right on the Black Top Highway.

The expertise of our employees, particularly our salespeople, has changed significantly over the years. In earlier days, knowledge of hunting and fishing were the exclusive areas of expertise, but today, of course, it has extended to every sort of outdoor leisure activity. Hunting and fishing remain the mainstays, and always will, but even if Justin Williams, the personification of the knowledgeable hunter/fisherman, was one of our reps today, he would be well versed in backpacking, bicycling and weekend camping. I'm not sure how he'd react to a request for color-coordinated hiking or skiing gear (he'd steer you to somebody who could help), but he'd certainly know about the type of hardware you needed. It would be interesting to see him in action in today's modern store, catering to so many varied tastes and needs.

Our huge variety of products can have unexpected benefits. One of our long-term sales reps was approached by a young couple in search of fishing gear, and he gives this amusing report of the transaction:

Rep: The man came up to me and said he wanted some clothes for fishing. I asked him what kind of fishing, and he said "fly fishing in streams," so I started out by showing him some waders. As we stood in front of the counter, the man and woman started talking, real loud. It seems the man loved fishing, but the woman hated it. Said she didn't even eat fish—couldn't stand it—so why go fishing. The man said it would be good exercise. Very relaxing for both of them. It would be fun. The woman wouldn't buy it and suggested that all they needed to do was go hiking. Well, here I am, with a couple pair of waders over my arms, and here's this argument going on, with people listening in, and I had to do something. So, I told the woman I'd show her some hiking clothes and backpacks and other stuff, and explain how to use them, and that maybe she could go hiking while her husband went fishing. That seemed to settle things down and I ended up outfitting her for the trail and him for the stream. They seemed happy enough as they walked out of the store, and I think Bean's saved a marriage by having what they both needed.

Another rep, overhearing this, said, "In this case, variety is the *splice* of life."

As I close this book, I want to say again that, in compiling my materials, the response to my questionnaires was remarkable. I thank you all. Very much! Without the time taken by Bean's old-line employees (and many newer ones) to fill the questionnaires out and contribute their anecdotes and comments, there is no way on earth this book could have been written. I have countless, unsolicited handwritten lines offering praise to the company, and it is this, more than anything else, that reveals the true nature and warmth of this unique and marvelous firm, and particularly of the wonderful people who work for it—the people I've written about.

This spirit of Bean's was caught in a brief editorial by Jim Wright in the *Dallas Morning News* of December 27, 1985:

> As the story in *The Dallas Morning News*' business section told it, large-bore executives from companies like Xerox and IBM have been trekking up to a little town in Maine to see how a rather low-tech mail-order company named L. L. Bean gets such fanatical loyalty from its customers and its employees. They try to discover the secret of this small-town dealer in boots, down coats and other outdoor gear.
>
> Actually, they could save the trip. Bean has never made any attempt to conceal its recipe for success, which is simply to treat its people—both customers and employees—like human beings instead of a disposable commodity.
>
> In an era when power plays and career strategies dominate the gladiatorial arenas of business, the little L. L. Bean company has grown into a giant just because it makes the people who buy from it and work for it feel appreciated. As a devout Bean's customer once put it, he was convinced that Bean was at least as intent on getting him just the right hiking boots for his backpacking trip as he was.

It's the kind of all-in-it-together feeling that can't be constructed with slick ad copy and gushy PR campaigns. And because most customer relations succeed or fail on the attitude of rank-and-file employees, the feeling has to permeate the whole organization, from board room to shop floor.

Amid all the talk about robotics, systems magic and productivity planning to make the United States competitive again in the global marketplace, it is very encouraging to see one American company that has become a world-beater with the simple, old-fashioned formula of trying to treat people decently.

L. L. would have liked that editorial.
He would have liked it very much indeed.

(Courtesy Andrew Freemire)

About the Author

*C*arlene Griffin (originally Carlene Groves) was born in Freeport, Maine, on February 11, 1917. She began working for L. L. Bean in 1935, when she was eighteen—and from here on it gets complicated.

Carlene left Bean's in 1936 to seek her fortune in Portland, returned to Bean's in 1942, married, and then left Bean's again to raise her children (four of them, in time), Jamie, Rand, Brett and Jim. She returned to Bean's for good in 1952 and has now been at the company steadily for 40 years. Her total time at Bean's adds up to 47 years.

As far as her work at Bean's is concerned, she has had so many different jobs with the company—from a dozen kinds of clerical duties to typing, inventory control, sales room rep and customer service—that even she is hazy about the specifics. She was assigned to the Telecommunications Department about three years ago and is currently in charge of a battery of twenty-four FAX machines.

Her first notion of writing a book about Bean's employees occurred about twenty years ago. But that was just a notion. Ten years ago, it became a serious notion, and about five years ago she started to do something about it, encouraged by her daughter, Jamie, who has also worked for Bean's.

On her 75th birthday, Carlene threw a ball for 750 guests and probably danced with a hundred of them. She goes to ". . . any amount of parties I can work in," and, not finding herself busy enough with a full-time job at Bean's, works five nights a week as a hostess at the Atrium hotel in nearby Brunswick.